GLENCOE

The American Journey
Early Years

Quizzes and Tests

Glencoe

To the Teacher

This *Quizzes and Tests* book offers section and chapter level assessment for *The American Journey: Early Years*. The book has been organized so that quizzes and tests appear at the point when you will most likely use them—the section quizzes followed by the chapter tests. Each quiz includes matching and short-answer questions. The tests include matching, multiple-choice, document-based, and essay questions.

Most classrooms have students with a wide variety of learning abilities. This book provides chapter tests to help you assess students who are at different learning levels. You will find three tests per chapter, each tailored to students who may function below, on, or above grade level. All of the tests are organized in the same format and are labeled A, B, and C.

> *Test, Form A*—for students functioning below grade level
> *Test, Form B*—for students functioning at grade level
> *Test, Form C*—for students functioning above grade level

The tests offer practical assessment of the chapter content, while providing differentiated instruction. They challenge students at all levels to recall key information, interpret primary source information, and practice writing skills.

A complete answer key appears at the back of this book. The answer key provides answers for every quiz and test in the order in which they appear in the book.

The **McGraw·Hill** Companies

 **Glencoe**

Send all inquiries to:
Glencoe/McGraw-Hill
8787 Orion Place
Columbus, OH 43240-4027

ISBN: 978-0-07-880677-3
MHID: 0-07-880677-1

Printed in the United States of America.

1 2 3 4 5 6 024 12 11 10 09 08

TABLE OF CONTENTS

Nationalism and Sectionalism

Civil War and Reconstruction

Section Quiz 1-1

Migration to the Americas

Matching   DIRECTIONS: Match each item in Column A with an item in Column B. Write the correct letter in each blank. *(10 points each)*

Column A

_____ **1.** things left behind by early people

_____ **2.** people who move from place to place

_____ **3.** movement of a group of people

_____ **4.** an early form of corn

_____ **5.** way to date artifacts

Column B

A. carbon dating

B. artifacts

C. maize

D. migration

E. nomads

Short Answer   DIRECTIONS: Answer each question below in the space provided. *(10 points each)*

6. Where do archaeologists believe early Americans came from?

_____

_____

7. What animal was a source of food for early hunters yet is not in existence today?

_____

_____

8. Why did early Americans come to the Americas?

_____

_____

9. During the Ice Age, what provided access to the Americas?

_____

_____

10. What development allowed the Native Americans to settle down?

_____

_____

1

Name_____ Date_____ Class_____

Score: _____

Section Quiz 1-2

Cities and Empires

Matching DIRECTIONS: Match each item in Column A with an item in Column B. Write the correct letter in each blank. *(10 points each)*

Column A

_____ **1.** society ruled by religious leaders

_____ **2.** a highly developed society

_____ **3.** builders of stone pyramids

_____ **4.** Inca capital city

_____ **5.** official Inca language

Column B

A. civilization

B. Cuzco

C. theocracy

D. Quechua

E. Maya

Short Answer DIRECTIONS: Answer each question below in the space provided. *(10 points each)*

6. What were Maya temples used for?

_____

_____

7. What was the form of writing the Maya created?

_____

_____

8. The Aztec capital of Tenochtitlán was built on an island in Lake Texcoco, which today is part of what city?

_____

_____

9. What was the string called that the Inca used to keep records?

_____

_____

10. What did the Inca make on steep slopes so that they could farm?

_____

_____

2

Score: _____

Section Quiz 1-3
North American Peoples

Matching   DIRECTIONS: Match each item in Column A with an item in Column B. Write the correct letter in each blank. *(10 points each)*

Column A

_____ **1.** cliff dwellers

_____ **2.** Mound Builders

_____ **3.** lived in hogans

_____ **4.** nomads

_____ **5.** desired peace

Column B

A. Iroquois

B. Plains peoples

C. Hopewell

D. Anasazi

E. Navajo

Short Answer   DIRECTIONS: Answer each question below in the space provided. *(10 points each)*

6. Which states make up the Four Corners?

_____

7. Which Native American group lived in the northernmost region in North America?

_____

8. The Mound Builders built mounds of earth that resembled what type of structure, constructed by which groups?

_____

_____

9. What is the name of the material made of sun-dried mud that the peoples of the Southwest used to construct their houses?

_____

10. A federation was first used by which Native American group? Why?

_____

_____

_____

3

Score: _____

Chapter 1 Test, Form A
The First Americans

Matching   DIRECTIONS: Match each item in Column A with an item in Column B. Write the correct letter in each blank. *(5 points each)*

Column A

_____ 1. broad platforms cut into mountains

_____ 2. government that links different groups

_____ 3. the study of ancient peoples

_____ 4. period of extreme cold

_____ 5. food source for early hunters

Column B

A. terraces

B. woolly mammoth

C. archaeology

D. ice age

E. federation

Multiple Choice   DIRECTIONS: In the blank, write the letter of the choice that best completes the statement or answers the question. *(8 points each)*

_____ 6. What was the capital of the Aztec Empire?
  A. Tikal
  B. Cuzco
  C. Tenochtitlán
  D. Chichén Itzá

_____ 7. Which was the largest of the early American civilizations?
  A. Olmec
  B. Maya
  C. Aztec
  D. Inca

_____ 8. Early Americans crossed the land bridge from Asia to present-day
  A. Oregon.
  B. Alaska.
  C. South America.
  D. Siberia.

_____ 9. The Aztec believed the gods required
  A. silver.
  B. animal sacrifice.
  C. human sacrifice.
  D. gold.

_____ 10. Tepees were used by which culture?
  A. peoples of the North
  B. peoples of the West
  C. peoples of the Plains
  D. peoples of the Southwest

Test, Form A (continued)

DBQ Document-Based Questions **DIRECTIONS:** Answer each question in the space provided. *(10 points each)*

> "You five great and powerful nations, with your tribes, must unite and have one common interest, and no foe shall disturb or subdue you. . . .
>
> "If we unite in one band, the Great Spirit will smile upon us and we shall be free, prosperous and happy. But if we shall remain as we are, we shall incur his displeasure. We shall be enslaved, and perhaps annihilated forever."

_____ **11.** This excerpt from a speech describes a group of eastern Native Americans' desire to join together in the

    A. Cahokia Treaty.

    B. Iroquois League.

    C. Great Peace.

    D. Cherokee Alliance.

_____ **12.** In the excerpt, what does the speaker say will happen to those tribes that unite?

    A. They will be enslaved and annihilated.

    B. They will win the war.

    C. They will be free, prosperous, and happy.

    D. They will subdue their foes.

Essay **DIRECTIONS:** Answer the following question on a separate sheet of paper. *(15 points)*

13. How and why did the early peoples come to the Americas?

Chapter 1 Test, Form B

The First Americans

Matching   DIRECTIONS: Match each item in Column A with an item in Column B. Write the correct letter in each blank. *(5 points each)*

Column A

_____ **1.** military empire

_____ **2.** built earthen pyramids

_____ **3.** sun-dried mud brick

_____ **4.** great stone community dwelling

_____ **5.** earliest civilization

Column B

A. Mound Builders

B. Aztec

C. pueblo

D. Olmec

E. adobe

Multiple Choice   DIRECTIONS: In the blank, write the letter of the choice that best completes the statement or answers the question. *(8 points each)*

_____ **6.** The earliest Native Americans crossed a land bridge called
   A. the Bering Strait.   **C.** Alaska.
   B. Atlantis.   **D.** Beringia.

_____ **7.** The Maya and the Aztec organized their societies around
   A. the military.   **C.** commerce.
   B. religion.   **D.** women.

_____ **8.** The largest settlement of Mound Builders was in present-day
   A. Ohio.   **C.** Mississippi.
   B. Illinois.   **D.** Indiana.

_____ **9.** In the 1500s, what changed the ways of life for Native Americans forever?
   A. climate changes   **C.** lack of food
   B. wars between nations   **D.** arrival of the Europeans

_____ **10.** Agriculture allowed early Americans to
   A. form communities.   **C.** form governments.
   B. hunt more efficiently.   **D.** travel farther.

Test, Form B (continued)

DBQ **Document-Based Questions** **DIRECTIONS:** Answer each question in the space provided. *(10 points each)*

> "Seneca, and you, the people who have your habitation at the foot of the Great Mountain and are overshadowed by its crags, shall be the third nation because you are all greatly gifted in speech.
>
> "Cayuga, you, whose dwelling is in the Dark Forest and whose home is everywhere, shall be the fourth nation because of your superior cunning in hunting.
>
> "Mohawk, and you, the people who live in the open country and possess much wisdom, shall be the fifth nation because you understand better the art of raising corn and beans and making cabins."
>
> —from the Founding Document of the Iroquois League

_____ **11.** How are the groups in the Iroquois League identified in this excerpt from a speech at its founding?

    A. by each group's traditional symbol

    B. by where they live and their best skill

    C. by the name of each group's chief

    D. by each group's kind of settlement

_____ **12.** Which answer best describes economic skills that were important to the peoples who lived in the woodlands of eastern North America?

    A. hunting and making war

    B. building cabins and herding animals

    C. hunting, farming, and building cabins

    D. planting and raising corn and beans

Essay **DIRECTIONS:** Answer the following question on a separate sheet of paper. *(15 points)*

13. How did different Native American groups adapt to their environment? Discuss at least three groups.

Chapter 1 Test, Form C

The First Americans

Matching   DIRECTIONS: Match each item in Column A with an item in Column B. Write the correct letter in each blank. *(5 points each)*

Column A

_____ **1.** believed to be descendant of the Inca sun god

_____ **2.** religious center of the Inca

_____ **3.** a system of record keeping with string

_____ **4.** group who dug irrigation channels

_____ **5.** used to farm on steep slopes

Column B

A. Hohokam

B. Machu Picchu

C. emperor

D. terraces

E. quipus

Multiple Choice   DIRECTIONS: In the blank, write the letter of the choice that best completes the statement or answers the question. *(8 points each)*

_____ **6.** What discovery turned nomads into farmers?

    A. clay   **C.** maize

    B. tomatoes   **D.** brick

_____ **7.** Mayan priests' interest in astronomy led to the creation of

    A. a 365-day calendar.   **C.** human sacrifices.

    B. a book of rules.   **D.** cave paintings.

_____ **8.** The Iroquois women who chose the male members of the Grand Council were called

    A. delegates.   **C.** clan mothers.

    B. group leaders.   **D.** family representatives.

_____ **9.** Which civilization built stone-paved roads over mountains?

    A. Inca   **C.** Aztec

    B. Maya   **D.** Olmec

_____ **10.** The Iroquois promoted peace by

    A. fighting a war.   **C.** signing a peace treaty.

    B. forming a war council.   **D.** forming a federation.

Test, Form C (continued)

DBQ **Document-Based Questions** **DIRECTIONS:** Answer each question in the space provided. *(10 points each)*

> "Friends and Brothers: You being members of many tribes, you have come from a great distance; the voice of war has aroused you up. You are afraid [for] your homes, your wives, and your children. You trembled for your safety. Believe me, I am with you. My heart beats with your hearts...
>
> "To oppose those hordes of northern tribes, singly and alone, would prove certain destruction.... We must unite ourselves into one common band of brothers. We must have but one voice. Many voices makes confusion. We must have one fire, one pipe, and one war club. This will give us strength. If our warriors are united, they can defeat the enemy and drive them from our land; if we do this, we are safe."
>
> —from the Founding Document of the Iroquois League

_____ **11.** Which statement best describes why the Native Americans in eastern North America decided to band together in the Iroquois League?

   A. These peoples would be stronger together in the League against their enemies.

   B. These peoples together in the League could drive all the Europeans away.

   C. These groups together in the League could conquer more territory.

   D. These peoples together in the League could raise more food and build big cities.

_____ **12.** Why do you think the speaker believed opposing the enemy singly would mean destruction?

   A. The speaker feared some people in the tribes would fight for the enemy if left alone.

   B. Each tribe would not have the supplies needed to combat the enemy alone.

   C. Separately the tribes were too small compared to the enemy.

   D. The enemy would have more opportunity to spy on the tribes.

Essay **DIRECTIONS:** Answer the following question on a separate sheet of paper. *(15 points)*

13. What was the legacy of the Iroquois that showed their desire for peace? Name the five nations that were part of their plan.

Score: _____

Section Quiz 2-1

A Changing World

Matching DIRECTIONS: Match each item in Column A with an item in Column B. Write the correct letter in each blank. *(10 points each)*

Column A

_____ **1.** Muslim house of worship

_____ **2.** ancient Greek and Roman works

_____ **3.** early navigation tool

_____ **4.** caravels

_____ **5.** journey to a holy place

Column B

A. classical

B. ships

C. pilgrimage

D. mosque

E. astrolabe

Short Answer DIRECTIONS: Answer each question below in the space provided. *(10 points each)*

6. Name the book that Marco Polo wrote to document his trip.

_____

_____

7. What does the word *Renaissance* mean in French?

_____

_____

8. What caused the growth of powerful nations in Europe?

_____

_____

9. How did Ghana prosper from trade?

_____

_____

10. What does the word *Renaissance* refer to?

_____

_____

Score: _____

Section Quiz 2-2
Early Exploration

Matching   DIRECTIONS: Match each item in Column A with an item in Column B. Write the correct letter in each blank. *(10 points each)*

Column A

_____ **1.** Viking sailor

_____ **2.** "Admiral of the Ocean Sea"

_____ **3.** leading explorers in the 1400s

_____ **4.** means "peaceful"

_____ **5.** to sail around the world

Column B

A. Pacific

B. circumnavigate

C. Leif Eriksson

D. Christopher Columbus

E. Portuguese

Short Answer   DIRECTIONS: Answer each question below in the space provided. *(10 points each)*

6. Why was exploration so important to Portugal?

_____

_____

7. What is a saga?

_____

_____

8. What made planning a journey difficult in the early days of exploration?

_____

_____

9. What did Henry the Navigator do?

_____

_____

10. Name two reasons Queen Isabella agreed to help Columbus financially.

_____

_____

Score: _____

Section Quiz 2-3

Spain in America

Matching DIRECTIONS: Match each item in Column A with an item in Column B. Write the correct letter in each blank. *(10 points each)*

Column A

_____ **1.** conquistadors

_____ **2.** Spanish upper class

_____ **3.** Spanish towns in the Americas

_____ **4.** Spanish religious communities

_____ **5.** Spanish Fort

Column B

A. pueblos

B. Spanish explorers

C. missions

D. *peninsulares*

E. presidio

Short Answer DIRECTIONS: Answer each question below in the space provided. *(10 points each)*

6. What is the Seven Cities of Cibola?

_____

_____

7. Name the first explorer who looked for the Seven Cities of Cibola.

_____

_____

8. How did Pizarro conquer the Inca Empire?

_____

_____

9. What did Bartolemé de Las Casas suggest that he later regretted?

_____

_____

10. What was the order of the Spanish class system?

_____

_____

Score: _____

Section Quiz 2-4

Exploring North America

Matching   DIRECTIONS: Match each item in Column A with an item in Column B. Write the correct letter in each blank. *(10 points each)*

Column A

_____ **1.** a German priest

_____ **2.** an economic theory

_____ **3.** established Quebec

_____ **4.** site of Montreal

_____ **5.** used for trade

Column B

A. royal mountain

B. Samuel de Champlain

C. beaver pelts

D. mercantilism

E. Martin Luther

Short Answer   DIRECTIONS: Answer each question below in the space provided. *(10 points each)*

6. Why did Martin Luther reject many Church practices?

_____

_____

7. Why did explorers hope to find the Northwest Passage?

_____

_____

8. What was the major way that religion affected the Americas?

_____

_____

9. What were the French trappers called?

_____

_____

10. How did the Protestant Reformation begin?

_____

_____

Score: _____

Chapter 2 Test, Form A

Exploring the Americas

Matching   DIRECTIONS: Match each item in Column A with an item in Column B. Write the correct letter in each blank. *(5 points each)*

Column A

_____ 1. to place upon something or someone

_____ 2. traditional story

_____ 3. narrow sea passage

_____ 4. a large estate

_____ 5. special privileges

Column B

A. strait

B. grants

C. saga

D. impose

E. plantation

Multiple Choice   DIRECTIONS: In the blank, write the letter of the choice that best completes the statement or answers the question. *(8 points each)*

_____ 6. The historical period of intellectual and artistic creativity is known as the

   A. Age of Enlightenment.   **C.** Middle Ages.

   B. Age of Reason.   **D.** Renaissance.

_____ 7. In 1492 Christopher Columbus sailed to America with the *Niña*, the *Pinta*, and the

   A. *Cortéz.*   **C.** *Santa María.*

   B. *Isabella.*   **D.** *Tordesillas.*

_____ 8. England, France, and the Netherlands hoped to discover a

   A. route to Africa.   **C.** southwest passage to India.

   B. route to South America.   **D.** northwest passage to Asia.

_____ 9. From their trading posts in Africa, the Portuguese traded for

   A. turquoise.   **C.** gold and slaves.

   B. tea.   **D.** salt.

_____ 10. Hernando de Soto traveled as far west as present-day

   A. Texas.   **C.** California.

   B. Oklahoma.   **D.** Oregon.

Test, Form A (continued)

DBQ Document-Based Questions **DIRECTIONS:** Answer the questions in the space provided. *(10 points each)*

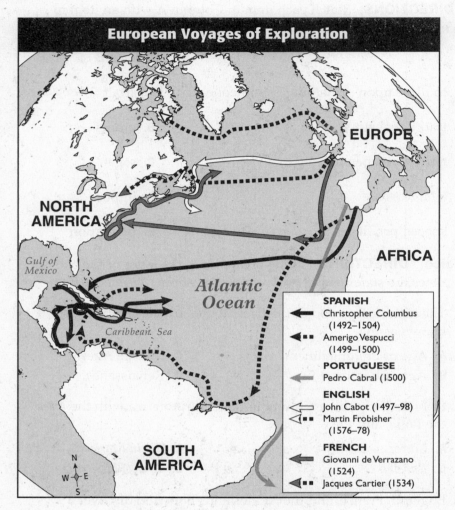

11. Of the explorers shown on the map, which two sailed on behalf of France?

   A. Cartier and Vespucci   **C.** Cartier and Verrazano

   B. Cabral and Verrazano   **D.** Vespucci and Cartier

12. Which explorer sailed the farthest west?

   A. Cabral   **C.** Vespucci

   B. Columbus   **D.** Frobisher

Essay DIRECTIONS: Answer the following question on a separate sheet of paper. *(15 points)*

13. How did the need for new trade routes lead to the discovery of the Americas?

Score: _____

Chapter 2 Test, Form B

Exploring the Americas

Matching DIRECTIONS: Match each item in Column A with an item in Column B. Write the correct letter in each blank. *(5 points each)*

Column A

_____ **1.** Inca ruler captured by Pizarro

_____ **2.** Mali's greatest king

_____ **3.** conquered the Aztec Empire

_____ **4.** Aztec emperor

_____ **5.** Henry Hudson's ship

Column B

A. Hernán Cortés

B. *Half Moon*

C. Mansa Mūsā

D. Montezuma

E. Athualpa

Multiple Choice DIRECTIONS: In the blank, write the letter of the choice that best completes the statement or answers the question. *(8 points each)*

_____ **6.** Which Portuguese prince laid the groundwork for a new era of exploration?

    A. Bartholomeu Dias

    B. Henry the Navigator

    C. John II

    D. Vasco da Gama

_____ **7.** Which Spaniard landed on the east coast of present-day Mexico in 1519?

    A. Juan Ponce de León

    B. Hernán Cortés

    C. Christopher Columbus

    D. Francisco Pizarro

_____ **8.** Which explorer founded Quebec?

    A. Champlain

    B. Cabot

    C. Cartier

    D. Joliet

_____ **9.** Which explorer discovered the long-awaited eastern sea route to Asia?

    A. Bartholomeu Dias

    B. Christopher Columbus

    C. Vasco da Gama

    D. Leif Eriksson

_____ **10.** Which explorer's crew was the first to sail around the world?

    A. Bartholomeu Dias's

    B. Juan Cabrillo's

    C. Christopher Columbus's

    D. Ferdinand Magellan's

Test, Form B (continued)

DBQ **Document-Based Questions** **DIRECTIONS:** Answer the questions in the space provided. *(10 points each)*

> ". . . I have decided upon writing you this letter to acquaint you with all the events which have occurred in my voyage, and the discoveries which have resulted from it. Thirty-three days after my departure from [Gomera] I reached the Indian Sea, where I discovered many islands, thickly peopled, of which I took possession without resistance in the name of our most illustrious monarch, by public proclamation and with unfurled banners."
>
> —Letter from Christopher Columbus to Lord Raphael Sanchez, March 1493

_____ 11. In this letter to one of his patrons, Columbus informs Sanchez that he has reached the sea near

   A. China.   **C.** America.

   B. Japan.   **D.** India.

_____ 12. When Columbus speaks of his "most illustrious monarch", to which royal figure is he referring?

   A. Prince Henry of Portugal   **C.** King John II of Portugal

   B. Queen Isabella of Spain   **D.** Alexander VI

Essay **DIRECTIONS:** Answer the following question on a separate sheet of paper. *(15 points)*

13. What were the reasons that Spain agreed to pay for Columbus's voyage?

Name_____ Date_____ Class_____

Chapter 2 Test, Form C
Exploring the Americas

Matching   DIRECTIONS: Match each item in Column A with an item in Column B. Write the correct letter in each blank. *(5 points each)*

Column A

_____ **1.** created a school of navigation

_____ **2.** explored the southernmost part of Africa

_____ **3.** completed the sea route to Asia

_____ **4.** destroyed the Inca in present-day Peru

_____ **5.** sailed around the world

Column B

A. Henry the Navigator

B. Vasco de Gama

C. Ferdinand Magellan

D. Francisco Pizarro

E. Bartholomeu Dias

Multiple Choice   DIRECTIONS: In the blank, write the letter of the choice that best completes the statement or answers the question. *(8 points each)*

_____ **6.** Who was Marco Polo?

A. a religious leader

B. a pirate

C. a philosopher

D. an explorer and author

_____ **7.** Who publicly condemned the cruel treatment of Native Americans by the Spanish?

A. Martin Luther

B. Bartolomé de Las Casas

C. Juana Inés de la Cruz

D. John Calvin

_____ **8.** What did the French want to establish in the Americas?

A. gold and silver mines

B. new communities

C. a fishing and fur trade

D. a slave trade

_____ **9.** The right granted by the Spanish government to the conquistadors that turned Native Americans into slaves was called

A. encomienda.

B. taxation.

C. Tordesillas.

D. presidio.

_____ **10.** Who believed that faith rather than good deeds was the way to salvation?

A. Martin Luther

B. Martin Buber

C. Bartolomé de las Casas

D. King Henry VIII

Test, Form C (continued)

DBQ **Document-Based Questions** **DIRECTIONS:** Answer the questions in the space provided. *(10 points each)*

> " . . . After nine days' march I reached some plains, so vast that I did not find their limit anywhere that I went, although I traveled over them for more than 300 leagues. And I found such a quantity of cows in these, of the kind that I wrote Your Majesty about, which they have in this country, that it is impossible to number them, for while I was journeying through these plains, until I returned to where I first found them, there was not a day that I lost sight of them. And after seventeen days' march I came to a settlement of Indians who are called Querechos, who travel around with these cows, who do not plant, and who eat the raw flesh and drink the blood of the cows they kill, and they tan the skins of the cows, with which all the people of this country dress themselves here. . . ."

_____ **11.** In this excerpt from a letter from the Spanish explorer, Coronado, to his king, the vast number of "cows" he mentions seeing were actually

    A. horses.   **C.** cattle.

    B. buffalo.   **D.** oxen.

_____ **12.** Coronado states that he reached a vast plain with strange "cows." Where in the United States did Coronado end up during this expedition to the West?

    A. New Mexico   **C.** Texas

    B. Arizona   **D.** Kansas

Essay **DIRECTIONS:** Answer the following question on a separate sheet of paper. *(15 points)*

13. What advances in technology paved the way for European voyages of exploration?

Score: _____

Section Quiz 3-1

Early English Settlements

Matching DIRECTIONS: Match each item in Column A with an item in Column B. Write the correct letter in each blank. *(10 points each)*

Column A

_____ 1. Sir Walter Raleigh's settlement

_____ 2. settlement named after the king

_____ 3. carved in a gatepost at Roanoke

_____ 4. claimed Newfoundland for Queen Elizabeth

_____ 5. husband of Pocahontas

Column B

A. Jamestown

B. Humphrey Gilbert

C. Roanoke

D. John Rolfe

E. *Croatoan*

Short Answer DIRECTIONS: Answer each question below in the space provided. *(10 points each)*

6. Who was given the right to claim land in North America by Queen Elizabeth?

_____

_____

7. What happened to the first 100 men who landed on Roanoke Island?

_____

_____

8. After the disaster at Roanoke, how many years did it take for the idea of creating colonies to reemerge?

_____

9. Who received the charter that created Jamestown?

_____

10. What happened to the colonists at Jamestown when John Smith left?

_____

_____

Score: _____

Section Quiz 3-2
New England Colonies

Matching DIRECTIONS: Match each item in Column A with an item in Column B. Write the correct letter in each blank. *(10 points each)*

Column A

_____ **1.** Squanto

_____ **2.** to treat harshly

_____ **3.** to disagree with

_____ **4.** *Mayflower's* passengers

_____ **5.** Metacomet

Column B

A. dissent

B. colonists' friend

C. King Philip

D. persecute

E. Pilgrims

Short Answer DIRECTIONS: Answer each question below in the space provided. *(10 points each)*

6. What became the new motivation to start a colony?

_____

_____

7. Who settled Rhode Island?

_____

8. Were the Separatists happy when they headed for the Netherlands? Why or why not?

_____

_____

9. What was the Mayflower Compact?

_____

_____

10. What did the Native Americans show the colonists that helped them survive?

_____

_____

Score: _____

Section Quiz 3-3
Middle Colonies

Matching   DIRECTIONS: Match each item in Column A with an item in Column B. Write the correct letter in each blank. *(10 points each)*

Column A

_____ 1. Governor of New Amsterdam in 1664

_____ 2. the Restoration

_____ 3. colony of New Netherland

_____ 4. a colony where the owner had control of all the land and the government

_____ 5. Society of Friends

Column B

A. Quakers

B. Charles II's reign

C. New Amsterdam

D. Peter Stuyvesant

E. proprietary colony

Short Answer   DIRECTIONS: Answer each question below in the space provided. *(10 points each)*

6. Why was New Amsterdam such a strong colony?

_____

_____

7. Which group of people helped found Pennsylvania?

_____

8. Which document granted colonists the right to elect representatives to the legislature of Pennsylvania?

_____

_____

9. What did the English rename the city of New Amsterdam?

_____

_____

10. The lower counties of Pennsylvania became known by what name?

_____

Score: _____

Section Quiz 3-4
Southern Colonies

Matching   DIRECTIONS: Match each item in Column A with an item in Column B. Write the correct letter in each blank. *(10 points each)*

Column A

Column B

_____ **1.** means "Charles's land"

A. Carolina

_____ **2.** plan of government

B. Louis Joliet

_____ **3.** people who can not pay their bills

C. constitution

_____ **4.** led a rebellion

D. Nathaniel Bacon

_____ **5.** a French fur trader and explorer

E. debtors

Short Answer   DIRECTIONS: Answer each question below in the space provided. *(10 points each)*

6. Did all the colonists come to America of their own free will?

_____

_____

7. What is an indentured servant?

_____

_____

8. What did Bacon's Rebellion show?

_____

_____

9. Did the colony of Georgia develop the way it was intended?

_____

_____

10. How long had Britain been in North America when Georgia was founded?

_____

_____

Score: _____

Chapter 3 Test, Form A
Colonial America

Matching **DIRECTIONS:** Match each item in Column A with an item in Column B. Write the correct letter in each blank. *(5 points each)*

Column A

_____ **1.** Jamestown legislative assembly

_____ **2.** Pilgrim colony

_____ **3.** colony that disappeared

_____ **4.** Pilgrim's ship

_____ **5.** religious settlements

Column B

A. Plymouth

B. *Mayflower*

C. missions

D. House of Burgesses

E. Roanoke

Multiple Choice **DIRECTIONS:** In the blank, write the letter of the choice that best completes the statement or answers the question. *(8 points each)*

_____ **6.** The Jamestown settlers found a way to make a profit for their investors by planting

    A. maize.
    B. cotton.
    C. tobacco.
    D. wheat.

_____ **7.** Protestants who wanted to leave the Anglican Church and found their own churches were called

    A. Protestant reformers.
    B. Anglicans.
    C. Separatists.
    D. Puritans.

_____ **8.** People who refuse to use force or fight in wars are called

    A. pacifists.
    B. pilgrims.
    C. reformers.
    D. patroons.

_____ **9.** Religious settlements established in California by the Spanish were called

    A. churches.
    B. missions.
    C. estates.
    D. retreats.

_____ **10.** Because their journey had a religious purpose, the Separatists called themselves

    A. Pilgrims.
    B. new colonists.
    C. Puritans.
    D. strangers.

Test, Form A (continued)

DBQ Document-Based Questions **DIRECTIONS:** Answer the questions in the space provided. *(10 points each)*

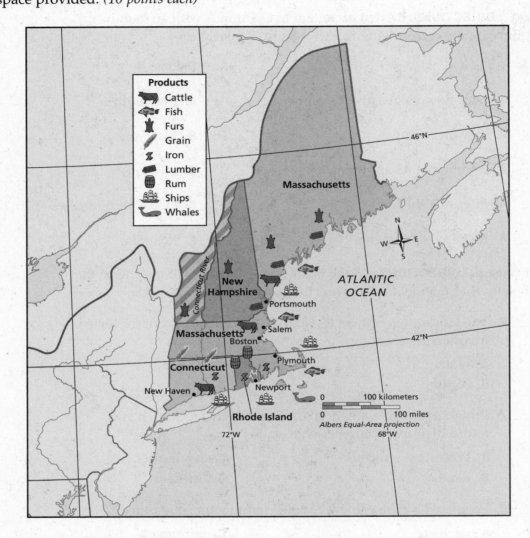

_____ **11.** According to the map, which group of products came from the New Hampshire colony?

A. furs, rum, iron

C. furs, lumber, cattle

B. furs, lumber, fish

D. furs, lumber, ships

_____ **12.** Which Northern colony is the smallest?

A. Maryland

C. Rhode Island

B. Plymouth

D. Connecticut

Essay DIRECTIONS: Answer the following question on a separate sheet of paper. *(15 points)*

13. Why did Carolina split into North Carolina and South Carolina?

Score: _____

Chapter 3 Test, Form B
Colonial America

Matching **DIRECTIONS:** Match each item in Column A with an item in Column B. Write the correct letter in each blank. *(5 points each)*

Column A

_____ **1.** Virginia's governor

_____ **2.** showed Pilgrims how to grow corn

_____ **3.** leader of Jamestown

_____ **4.** "city of brotherly love"

_____ **5.** site of Spanish military post

Column B

A. Captain John Smith

B. San Antonio

C. Sir William Berkeley

D. Squanto

E. Philadelphia

Multiple Choice **DIRECTIONS:** In the blank, write the letter of the choice that best completes the statement or answers the question. *(8 points each)*

_____ **6.** Puritans formed the Massachusetts Bay Company and received a royal charter to establish a colony north of

    A. Plymouth.   **C.** Boston.

    B. Mayflower.   **D.** Rhode Island.

_____ **7.** Which law granted the right to worship freely in Maryland?

    A. Charter of Privileges   **C.** Fundamental Orders

    B. Act of Toleration   **D.** Maryland constitution

_____ **8.** Who claimed Newfoundland for Queen Elizabeth?

    A. Francis Drake   **C.** Sir Humphrey Gilbert

    B. John White   **D.** Sir Walter Raleigh

_____ **9.** Which group maintained the friendliest relations with the Native Americans?

    A. the Spanish   **C.** the English

    B. the Dutch   **D.** the French

_____ **10.** The last of the British colonies to be established in America was

    A. Maryland.   **C.** Pennsylvania.

    B. Carolina.   **D.** Georgia.

Test, Form B (continued)

DBQ **Document-Based Questions** **DIRECTIONS:** Answer the questions in the space provided. *(10 points each)*

On September 6, 1620, the *Mayflower* left for America. It landed in America on November 11, 1620. The ship's passengers were Pilgrims and English colonists who were not Pilgrims. These English colonists were called "strangers" by Governor Bradford.

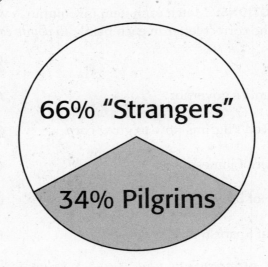

66% "Strangers"

34% Pilgrims

11. Which group made up the majority of the passengers, Pilgrims or "strangers"? By how much?

_____

_____

_____

12. Who were the "strangers"?

_____

_____

_____

Essay **DIRECTIONS:** Answer the following question on a separate sheet of paper. *(15 points)*

13. What were some of the hardships the colonists faced in America?

Score: _____

Chapter 3 Test, Form C
Colonial America

Matching **DIRECTIONS:** Match each item in Column A with an item in Column B. Write the correct letter in each blank. *(5 points each)*

Column A

_____ 1. first written constitution in America

_____ 2. also known as King Philip

_____ 3. Jamestown colony stockholders

_____ 4. carved on a gatepost at Roanoke

_____ 5. wealthy landowners

Column B

A. patroons

B. Fundamental Orders of Connecticut

C. *Croatoan*

D. Metacomet

E. General Court

Multiple Choice **DIRECTIONS:** In the blank, write the letter of the choice that best completes the statement or answers the question. *(8 points each)*

_____ 6. What did King James I grant groups of merchants to organize settlements in America?

  A. stocks   **C.** pledges
  B. compacts   **D.** charters

_____ 7. Who wrote Pennsylvania's first constitution?

  A. William Penn   **C.** Oliver Cromwell
  B. Sir George Carteret   **D.** Peter Stuyvesant

_____ 8. Which document covered land divisions and social ranking?

  A. Georgia Agreement   **C.** Pennsylvania Compact
  B. Delaware Declaration **D.** Carolina constitution

_____ 9. The English sent a fleet to attack and acquire which colony in 1664?

  A. New Netherland   **C.** Manhattan
  B. Philadelphia   **D.** New Amsterdam

_____ 10. Which law protected Catholics from any attempt to make Maryland a Protestant colony?

  A. Catholic Reformation **C.** the Maryland Law
  B. Act of Toleration   **D.** Law of Religious Freedom

Test, Form C (continued)

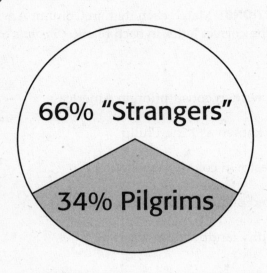

DBQ **Document-Based Questions** **DIRECTIONS:** Answer the questions in the space provided. (10 points each)

On September 6, 1620, the *Mayflower* left for America. It landed in America on November 11, 1620. The ship's passengers were Pilgrims and English colonists who were not Pilgrims. These English colonists were called "strangers" by Governor Bradford.

66% "Strangers"

34% Pilgrims

11. Why do you think Governor Bradford called passengers who were not Pilgrims "strangers"?

_____

_____

_____

12. How much time did the *Mayflower*'s voyage take?

_____

_____

_____

Essay **DIRECTIONS:** Answer the following question on a separate sheet of paper. (15 points)

13. Who were the Pilgrims and why did they use that name?

Copyright © Glencoe/McGraw-Hill, a division of The McGraw-Hill Companies, Inc.

Score: _____

Section Quiz 4-1
Life in the Colonies

Matching   DIRECTIONS: Match each item in Column A with an item in Column B. Write the correct letter in each blank. *(10 points each)*

Column A

_____ 1. a piece of land that faced the meetinghouse

_____ 2. crops that sold easily

_____ 3. cultural variety

_____ 4. near Appalachian Mountains

_____ 5. governed slaves

Column B

A. cash crops

B. backcountry

C. slave codes

D. common

E. diversity

Short Answer   DIRECTIONS: Answer each question below in the space provided. *(10 points each)*

6. What was the major crop grown in South Carolina and Georgia?

_____

7. Name three reasons the colonies started to grow quickly in population.

_____

_____

8. Name examples of chores a child would have on a colonial farm.

_____

_____

9. What were the slave codes?

_____

_____

10. Why did the Navigation Acts anger colonists?

_____

_____

Section Quiz 4-2

Government, Religion, Culture

Matching   DIRECTIONS: Match each item in Column A with an item in Column B. Write the correct letter in each blank. *(10 points each)*

Column A

_____ **1.** economic theory

_____ **2.** trading illegally

_____ **3.** royal colonies

_____ **4.** period of political change in England

_____ **5.** learning assistant to a craft worker

Column B

A. ruled by Britain

B. Glorious Revolution

C. smuggling

D. apprentice

E. mercantilism

Short Answer   DIRECTIONS: Answer each question below in the space provided. *(10 points each)*

6. Who were William and Mary?

_____

_____

7. What was England's view on the North American colonies?

_____

_____

8. What concepts did the Magna Carta instill in the colonists?

_____

_____

9. Name three things that contributed to American culture.

_____

_____

10. What legal case was an important step toward the idea of freedom of the press?

_____

_____

Section Quiz 4-3

France and Britain Clash

Matching **DIRECTIONS:** Match each item in Column A with an item in Column B. Write the correct letter in each blank. *(10 points each)*

Column A

_____ **1.** British fort

_____ **2.** French fortress

_____ **3.** powerful group of Native Americans

_____ **4.** a surveyor sent to warn the French

_____ **5.** outpost established by Washington

Column B

A. Iroquois Confederacy

B. Fort Necessity

C. Louisbourg

D. Pickawillany

E. George Washington

Short Answer **DIRECTIONS:** Answer each question below in the space provided. *(10 points each)*

6. What did the English call the Iroquois Confederacy?

_____

_____

7. Why did the Albany Plan of Union fail?

_____

_____

8. Why were the French and the Native Americans allies?

_____

_____

9. Which countries were the major powers in North America?

_____

_____

10. What did Washington's troops discover in the Ohio River valley?

_____

_____

Score: _____

Section Quiz 4-4

The French and Indian War

Matching   DIRECTIONS: Match each item in Column A with an item in Column B. Write the correct letter in each blank. *(10 points each)*

Column A

_____ 1. one of Edward Braddock's aides

_____ 2. Britain's prime minister

_____ 3. conquered Quebec

_____ 4. conquered Montreal

_____ 5. united the Native Americans

Column B

A. James Wolfe

B. George Washington

C. Pontiac

D. William Pitt

E. Jeffrey Amherst

Short Answer   DIRECTIONS: Answer each question below in the space provided. *(10 points each)*

6. Name several elements of the struggle between Britain and France besides the French and Indian war.

_____

_____

_____

7. What did the Treaty of Paris force France to do in North America?

_____

_____

8. What happened after William Pitt became prime minister in England?

_____

_____

9. What army strategy did Washington warn Braddock about?

_____

_____

10. What was Pitt's plan to deal with the cost of the war?

_____

_____

Score: _____

Chapter 4 Test, Form A
Growth of the Thirteen Colonies

Matching   DIRECTIONS: Match each item in Column A with an item in Column B. Write the correct letter in each blank. *(5 points each)*

Column A

_____ **1.** laws that governed slaves

_____ **2.** first college in the United States

_____ **3.** main cash crop in Georgia

_____ **4.** written by Benjamin Franklin

_____ **5.** clash between the French and British that started in 1756

Column B

A. Albany Plan of Union

B. Harvard

C. rice

D. Seven Years' War

E. slave codes

Multiple Choice   DIRECTIONS: In the blank, write the letter of the choice that best completes the statement or answers the question. *(8 points each)*

_____ **6.** A group of civilians trained to fight in emergencies is

   A. a militia.

   B. an army.

   C. a confederacy.

   D. a commando.

_____ **7.** The religious revival that swept through the colonies was called the

   A. Enlightenment.

   B. Great Migration.

   C. Great Awakening.

   D. Catholic Revolution.

_____ **8.** In the Southern Colonies, the region of small farms was called the

   A. Tidewater.

   B. backcountry.

   C. mountainous region.

   D. coastal area.

_____ **9.** The Treaty of Paris marked the end of power in North America for

   A. Britain.

   B. Canada.

   C. France.

   D. Spain.

_____ **10.** The leg of the triangular trade route in which enslaved Africans were shipped to the West Indies was known as the

   A. Tidewater.

   B. Slave Code.

   C. First Leg.

   D. Middle Passage.

Test, Form A (continued)

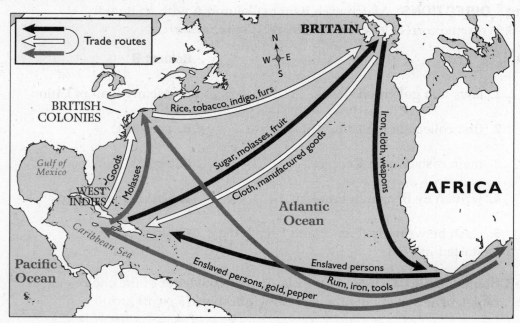

DBQ **Document-Based Questions** **DIRECTIONS:** Answer each question in the space provided. *(10 points each)*

_____ 11. According to the trade routes map, what besides enslaved people was imported to the New World from Africa?

    A. iron, tools   **C.** corn, furs

    B. gold, pepper   **D.** rice, tobacco

_____ 12. Pick the best title for the map from the choices below.

    A. National Origins of Colonists   **C.** European Settlement Patterns

    B. The Great Awakening   **D.** Triangular Trade Routes

Essay **DIRECTIONS:** Answer the following question on a separate sheet of paper. *(15 points)*

13. What was the triangular trade?

Score: _____

Chapter 4 Test, Form B
Growth of the Thirteen Colonies

Matching   DIRECTIONS: Match each item in Column A with an item in Column B. Write the correct letter in each blank. *(5 points each)*

Column A

_____ **1.** region of large Southern plantations

_____ **2.** directed trade between England and the colonies

_____ **3.** powerful group of Native Americans

_____ **4.** halted westward expansion

_____ **5.** religious revival

Column B

A. Iroquois Confederacy

B. Great Awakening

C. Navigation Acts

D. Tidewater

E. Proclamation of 1763

Multiple Choice   DIRECTIONS: In the blank, write the letter of the choice that best completes the statement or answers the question. *(8 points each)*

_____ **6.** The type of farming practiced in New England was
  A. subsistence.   **C.** cash crop.
  B. Tidewater.   **D.** backwater.

_____ **7.** The most profitable cash crop in South Carolina and Georgia was
  A. corn.   **C.** rice.
  B. lumber.   **D.** tobacco.

_____ **8.** Which leader recognized that British settlers threatened the Native Americans' way of life?
  A. Buick   **C.** Pontiac
  B. Detroit   **D.** Ottawa

_____ **9.** Which plan called for one general government for all of the American colonies?
  A. Iroquois Confederacy   **C.** Glorious Revolution
  B. Albany Plan of Union   **D.** Proclamation of 1763

_____ **10.** Which British commander was sent to conquer the French in the Ohio River valley?
  A. Jonathan Edwards   **C.** George Washington
  B. George Whitefield   **D.** Edward Braddock

Test, Form B (continued)

DBQ Document-Based Questions DIRECTIONS: Answer each question in the space provided. *(10 points each)*

Colonial Expansion		
War	Years	Causes
King William's War	1689–1697	French and Native American allies attacked the English and the colonists
Queen Anne's War	1702–1713	French and Native Americans attacked New England Colonies
King George's War	1744–1748	French and British fought in New England

_____ **11.** According to the chart, how many years elapsed between the end of Queen Anne's War and the beginning of King George's War?

    A. 31   **C.** 41

    B. 39   **D.** 44

_____ **12.** Which group was involved in every war mentioned in the chart?

    A. British   **C.** Native Americans

    B. the colonists   **D.** the French

Essay DIRECTIONS: Answer the following question on a separate sheet of paper. *(15 points)*

13. What were the three types of colonies? Describe one type.

Score: _____

Chapter 4 Test, Form C
Growth of the Thirteen Colonies

Matching   DIRECTIONS: Match each item in Column A with an item in Column B. Write the correct letter in each blank. *(5 points each)*

Column A

_____ **1.** British commander

_____ **2.** Ottawa chief

_____ **3.** oversaw the war effort from London

_____ **4.** important New England industry

_____ **5.** civilian soldiers

Column B

A. militia

B. Jeffrey Amherst

C. Pontiac

D. shipbuilding

E. William Pitt

Multiple Choice   DIRECTIONS: In the blank, write the letter of the choice that best completes the statement or answers the question. *(8 points each)*

_____ **6.** How did England view its North American colonies?

  A. as an economic drain
  B. as a land of savages
  C. as an economic resource
  D. as a place to send criminals

_____ **7.** Who exemplified the Enlightenment?

  A. George Whitefield
  B. George Washington
  C. Jonathan Edwards
  D. Benjamin Franklin

_____ **8.** Which proposal sought to unite the American colonies against the French?

  A. Albany Plan of Union
  B. Confederacy of England
  C. United States Constitution
  D. Bill of Rights

_____ **9.** The Seven Years' War was a war between

  A. Spain and Britain.
  B. France and Spain.
  C. France and Native Americans.
  D. France and Britain.

_____ **10.** Which theory holds that a nation's power depends on expanding its trade?

  A. mercantilism
  B. trade
  C. gold reserve
  D. expansion

✓ Test, Form C (continued)

DBQ **Document-Based Questions** **DIRECTIONS:** Answer the question in the space provided. *(10 points each)*

> "Our German Society have in this place now established a lucrative trade in woolen and linen goods, together with a large assortment of other useful and necessary articles, and have entrusted this extensive business to my own direction. Besides this they have now purchased and hold over 30,000 acres of land, for the sake of establishing an entirely German colony. In my newly laid out Germantown there are already sixty-four families in a very prosperous condition. Such persons, therefore, and all those who still arrive, have to fall to work and swing the axe most vigorously; for wherever you turn the cry is, *Itur in antiquam sylvam* [Let us go through the primeval forest], nothing but endless forests."

_____ **11.** According to this excerpt from a letter in 1700, how are the settlers of Germantown proceeding to set up their colony?

   A. They are starting businesses and working hard to clear the forest.
   B. They have built a fort and are waiting for supplies to arrive.
   C. They are trading profitably with the Native Americans near them.
   D. They have started a strict religious community and built a cathedral.

12. What might the German colonies need to overcome to continue to grow?

_____

_____

Essay **DIRECTIONS:** Answer the following question on a separate sheet of paper. *(15 points)*

13. Why did the Middle Colonies have more tolerance for religious and cultural differences than the New England Colonies?

Score: _____

Section Quiz 5-1

Taxation Without Representation

Matching DIRECTIONS: Match each item in Column A with an item in Column B. Write the correct letter in each blank. *(10 points each)*

Column A

_____ **1.** incoming money

_____ **2.** formal expression of opinion

_____ **3.** rag figures

_____ **4.** British prime minister who decided to act against smuggling

_____ **5.** to refuse to buy

Column B

A. George Grenville

B. effigies

C. revenue

D. boycott

E. resolution

Short Answer DIRECTIONS: Answer each question below in the space provided. *(10 points each)*

6. What are writs of assistance?

_____

_____

7. What was the purpose of the Stamp Act Congress?

_____

_____

8. What did the Proclamation of 1763 accomplish?

_____

_____

9. What did Parliament do after it repealed the Stamp Act?

_____

_____

10. How did the colonists react to the taxes being imposed by Britain?

_____

_____

Score: _____

Section Quiz 5-2
Building Colonial Unity

Matching   DIRECTIONS: Match each item in Column A with an item in Column B. Write the correct letter in each blank. *(10 points each)*

Column A

_____ 1. participant in Boston Tea Party

_____ 2. ruler of Britain

_____ 3. circulated colonists' grievances

_____ 4. closed Boston Harbor

_____ 5. information made to influence public opinion

Column B

A. propaganda

B. committee of correspondence

C. Coercive Acts

D. Samuel Adams

E. George III

Short Answer   DIRECTIONS: Answer each question below in the space provided. *(10 points each)*

6. How did Parliament react to the Boston Massacre?

_____

_____

7. Which organization did Samuel Adams revive after the Boston Massacre?

_____

_____

8. What were some events or issues that encouraged the Boston Massacre?

_____

_____

9. What was the result of closing Boston Harbor under the Coercive Acts?

_____

_____

10. Why did the colonists consider the Coercive Acts intolerable?

_____

_____

Section Quiz 5-3
A Call to Arms

Matching **DIRECTIONS:** Match each item in Column A with an item in Column B. Write the correct letter in each blank. *(10 points each)*

Column A

_____ **1.** citizen soldiers

_____ **2.** storage place for arms

_____ **3.** the man who rode with Paul Revere

_____ **4.** warned that the British were coming

_____ **5.** sold military information to the British

Column B

A. Paul Revere

B. militias

C. Benedict Arnold

D. Concord

E. William Dawes

Short Answer **DIRECTIONS:** Answer each question below in the space provided. *(10 points each)*

6. What instructions did Thomas Gage have regarding the colonists?

_____

_____

7. Who led the minutemen in the first battle against the British?

_____

_____

8. What were the Suffix Resolves?

_____

_____

9. Where did the victory of the Green Mountain Boys take place?

_____

_____

10. What did the British learn at the Battle of Bunker Hill?

_____

_____

Name_____ Date_____ Class_____

Section Quiz 5-4
Moving Toward Independence

Matching DIRECTIONS: Match each item in Column A with an item in Column B. Write the correct letter in each blank. *(10 points each)*

Column A

Column B

_____ **1.** president of the Congress

A. Thomas Paine

_____ **2.** governed the colonies

B. Charles Inglis

_____ **3.** wrote *Common Sense*

C. Second Continental Congress

_____ **4.** argued against going to war with Britain

D. Thomas Jefferson

_____ **5.** wrote the Declaration of Independence

E. John Hancock

Short Answer DIRECTIONS: Answer each question below in the space provided. *(10 points each)*

6. What philosopher did Jefferson use for inspiration?

_____

_____

7. Who was the president of the Second Continental Congress?

_____

_____

8. What are some of the ideas that Locke presents in his philosophy?

_____

_____

9. On what date was the resolution for independence voted and approved?

_____

_____

10. How many delegates signed the Declaration of Independence?

_____

_____

Score: _____

Chapter 5 Test, Form A

The Spirit of Independence

Matching   DIRECTIONS: Match each item in Column A with an item in Column B. Write the correct letter in each blank. *(5 points each)*

Column A

_____ **1.** benefited from the Tea Act

_____ **2.** preamble

_____ **3.** legal document permitting searches

_____ **4.** victim of Boston Massacre

_____ **5.** writer of "The Concord Hymn"

Column B

A. East India Company

B. Crispus Attucks

C. writ of assistance

D. Ralph Waldo Emerson

E. introduction

Multiple Choice   DIRECTIONS: In the blank, write the letter of the choice that best completes the statement or answers the question. *(8 points each)*

_____ **6.** The British government tried to stop smuggling with the
- **A.** Stamp Act.
- **B.** Molasses Act.
- **C.** Sugar Act.
- **D.** Trade Act.

_____ **7.** Which act taxed almost all printed material in the colonies?
- **A.** Sugar Act
- **B.** Stamp Act
- **C.** Iron Act
- **D.** Hat Act

_____ **8.** The man who wrote the Declaration of Independence was
- **A.** Thomas Jefferson.
- **B.** Patrick Henry.
- **C.** Benjamin Franklin.
- **D.** John Adams.

_____ **9.** Who ran the first post office established by the Second Continental Congress?
- **A.** John Adams
- **B.** Benjamin Franklin
- **C.** Thomas Jefferson
- **D.** George Washington

_____ **10.** Which colonists wanted to fight the British for American independence?
- **A.** Loyalists
- **B.** Patriots
- **C.** Separatists
- **D.** Nationalists

✓ Test, Form A (continued)

DBO Document-Based Questions DIRECTIONS: Answer the questions in the space provided. *(10 points each)*

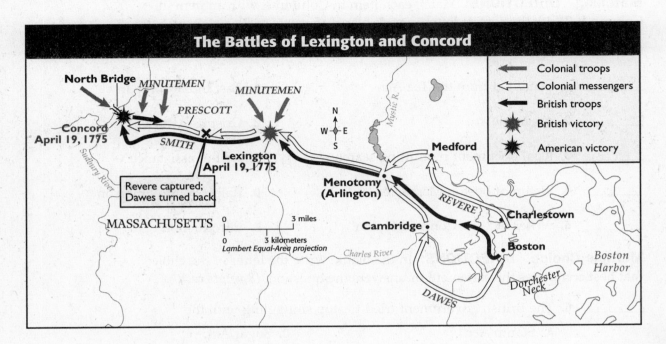

The Battles of Lexington and Concord

_____ **11.** In which state were the battles of Lexington and Concord fought?

    A. New Hampshire   **C.** Rhode Island

    B. Connecticut   **D.** Massachusetts

_____ **12.** The battles of Lexington and Concord were fought

    A. on the same day.   **C.** three days apart.

    B. at the same exact location.   **D.** one month apart.

Essay DIRECTIONS: Answer the following question on a separate sheet of paper. *(15 points)*

13. What did the First Continental Congress decide?

Score: _____

Chapter 5 Test, Form B

The Spirit of Independence

Matching   DIRECTIONS: Match each item in Column A with an item in Column B. Write the correct letter in each blank. *(5 points each)*

Column A

Column B

_____ 1. prevented supplies from being shipped to Boston

_____ 2. Patriot leader

_____ 3. persuaded the burgesses to take action against the Stamp Act

_____ 4. organized the Sons of Liberty

_____ 5. shouted "The regulars are out!"

A. Intolerable Acts

B. Patrick Henry

C. Paul Revere

D. William Prescott

E. Samuel Adams

Multiple Choice   DIRECTIONS: In the blank, write the letter of the choice that best completes the statement or answers the question. *(8 points each)*

_____ 6. The Proclamation of 1763 prohibited colonists from moving west of the

    A. Louisiana Territory.

    B. Ohio River valley.

    C. Appalachian Mountains.

    D. Great Lakes.

_____ 7. Who led the Green Mountain Boys?

    A. Ethan Allen

    B. Sam Adams

    C. Ben Franklin

    D. Paul Revere

_____ 8. Who refused to receive the Olive Branch Petition?

    A. William Dawes

    B. George III

    C. Thomas Jefferson

    D. Thomas Gage

_____ 9. "The shot heard 'round the world" refers to the actions of the minutemen at

    A. Bunker Hill.

    B. Breed's Hill.

    C. Lexington and Concord.

    D. Boston.

_____ 10. Who wrote *Common Sense*?

    A. Thomas Paine

    B. John Adams

    C. Benjamin Franklin

    D. Thomas Jefferson

Test, Form B (continued)

DBQ **Document-Based Questions** **DIRECTIONS:** Answer the questions in the space provided. (*10 points each*)

Paul Revere's Silver Business				
	Period A 1761–1775		Period B 1779–1797	
Silver Objects	**Number**	**Percent**	**Number**	**Percent**
Flatware	410	35.8	2,069	49.15
Tea and Coffee Wares	61	5.3	198	4.7
Tablewares	129	11.3	177	4.2
Personal Items	449	39.2	623	14.8
Harness Fittings	0	0.0	1,044	24.8
Miscellaneous	96	8.4	99	2.35
Total Objects	1,145	100.0	4,210	100.0

_____ **11.** According to the table, what did silversmith Paul Revere's business produce in Period B that it did not produce in Period A?

    A. flatware   **C.** harness fittings

    B. tablewares   **D.** miscellaneous

_____ **12.** According to the table, about five times more of one thing was produced in Period B than in Period A. What was it?

    A. flatware   **C.** personal items

    B. tablewares   **D.** harness fittings

Essay **DIRECTIONS:** Answer the following question on a separate sheet of paper. (*15 points*)

13. What was the significance of the Boston Tea Party?

Score: _____

Chapter 5 Test, Form C
The Spirit of Independence

Matching   DIRECTIONS: Match each item in Column A with an item in Column B. Write the correct letter in each blank. *(5 points each)*

Column A

_____ 1. taxed printed material

_____ 2. made propaganda posters

_____ 3. united protesters opposed to British rule

_____ 4. proposed that the colonies be free

_____ 5. leader of minutemen

Column B

A. committees of correspondence

B. Samuel Adams

C. Stamp Act

D. Captain John Parker

E. Richard Henry Lee

Multiple Choice   DIRECTIONS: In the blank, write the letter of the choice that best completes the statement or answers the question. *(8 points each)*

_____ 6. The king and Parliament viewed the American colonies as a

   A. place for vacations.   **C.** source of irritation.
   B. drain on their economy.   **D.** source of funds.

_____ 7. Who persuaded the House of Burgesses to take action against the Stamp Act?

   A. Patrick Henry   **C.** John Adams
   B. Samuel Adams   **D.** Benjamin Franklin

_____ 8. Which act gave the British Parliament the right to tax and make decisions for the colonies "in all cases"?

   A. Sugar Act   **C.** Stamp Act
   B. Townshend Acts   **D.** Declaratory Act

_____ 9. Which colonists did not consider unfair taxes a good reason for rebellion?

   A. Separatists   **C.** Patriots
   B. Nationalists   **D.** Loyalists

_____ 10. George Washington was chosen commander of the Continental Army upon the recommendation of

   A. Sam Adams.   **C.** John Adams.
   B. Thomas Gage.   **D.** Ben Franklin.

Test, Form C (continued)

DBQ Document-Based Questions **DIRECTIONS:** Answer the questions in the space provided. *(10 points each)*

> "I challenge the warmest advocate for reconciliation to show a single advantage that this continent can reap, by being connected with Great Britain. I repeat the challenge, not a single advantage is derived. Our corn will fetch its price in any market in Europe, and our imported goods must be paid for, buy them where we will.
> "But the injuries and disadvantages we sustain by that connection are without number; and our duty to mankind at large, as well as to ourselves, instructs us to renounce the alliance: because any submission to, or dependence on, Great Britain, tends directly to involve this continent in European wars and quarrels, and sets us at variance with nations who would otherwise seek our friendship, and against whom we have neither anger nor complaint. . . ."
>
> —*Common Sense*, 1776

_____ **11.** The arguments for American independence written in *Common Sense* by _____ greatly influenced colonists' opinions.

   A. Thomas Jefferson   **C.** Patrick Henry

   B. Charles Inglis   **D.** Thomas Paine

_____ **12.** The author of this passage thinks America's involvement with Britain causes

   A. growth of American industry.

   B. strength in the relationship that has already been established.

   C. unneeded differences with European nations that could become allies.

   D. many advantages that colonists can not turn down.

Essay   DIRECTIONS: Answer the following question on a separate sheet of paper. *(15 points)*

13. Why did the Stamp Act cause more resistance among ordinary people in the colonies than did the Sugar Act?

Score: _____

Section Quiz 6-1

The Early Years

Matching   DIRECTIONS: Match each item in Column A with an item in
Column B. Write the correct letter in each blank. *(10 points each)*

Column A

_____ **1.** American supporters of independence

_____ **2.** taking neither side

_____ **3.** Loyalists

_____ **4.** mercenaries

_____ **5.** to recruit

Column B

A. Tories

B. Patriots

C. enlist

D. neutral

E. hired soldiers

Short Answer   DIRECTIONS: Answer each question below in the space
provided. *(10 points each)*

6. Name two types of soldiers who helped the British.

_____

7. What did Lord Dunmore do to help the British attract more soldiers?

_____

_____

8. Why was it difficult for America to raise an army?

_____

_____

9. What was a low point for the Patriots' army?

_____

10. How did the British hope to gain victory in 1777?

_____

_____

Name_____ Date_____ Class_____

Matching DIRECTIONS: Match each item in Column A with an item in Column B. Write the correct letter in each blank. *(10 points each)*

Column A

_____ **1.** General Howe's winter camp

_____ **2.** French noble at Valley Forge

_____ **3.** fled the colonies

_____ **4.** leaving the army without permission

_____ **5.** stood up for women's interests

Column B

A. deserting

B. Abigail Adams

C. Loyalists

D. the Marquis de Lafayette

E. Philadelphia

Short Answer DIRECTIONS: Answer each question below in the space provided. *(10 points each)*

6. In 1778 where did the Continental Army spend its harshest winter?

_____

7. How did Friedrich von Steuben help the army?

_____

_____

8. What happened when the Congress and the states both printed money?

_____

_____

9. Who argued that a woman's mind is as good as a man's?

_____

_____

10. What happened to Loyalists during the war?

_____

_____

Score: _____

Section Quiz 6-3

The War Moves West and South

Matching   DIRECTIONS: Match each item in Column A with an item in Column B. Write the correct letter in each blank. *(10 points each)*

Column A

_____ **1.** privately owned warships

_____ **2.** surrendered to John Paul Jones

_____ **3.** the British post seized by the Americans

_____ **4.** worst American defeat of the war

_____ **5.** American victory in September 1780

Column B

A. Kaskaskia

B. Charles Town

C. privateers

D. Kings Mountain

E. *Serapis*

Short Answer   DIRECTIONS: Answer each question below in the space provided. *(10 points each)*

6. What was the worst American defeat of the war?

_____

7. What is a privateer?

_____

_____

8. Who was known as "the hair buyer" and why?

_____

_____

9. How was Bernardo de Gálvez important to American success in the war?

_____

_____

10. What did Cornwallis do in Virginia?

_____

_____

Score: _____

Section Quiz 6-4
The War Is Won

Matching   DIRECTIONS: Match each item in Column A with an item in Column B. Write the correct letter in each blank. *(10 points each)*

Column A

_____ **1.** French commander

_____ **2.** British commander at Yorktown

_____ **3.** French naval commander who assisted Cornwallis at Yorktown

_____ **4.** to approve

_____ **5.** a surprise attack

Column B

A. ratify

B. Comte de Rochambeau

C. François de Grasse

D. Charles Cornwallis

E. ambush

Short Answer   DIRECTIONS: Answer each question below in the space provided. *(10 points each)*

6. Did Washington's plan for Yorktown work? Why or why not?

_____

_____

7. Who went to Paris to sign the treaty?

_____

8. What was the American strategy at Yorktown?

_____

_____

9. Name two terms of the Treaty of Paris.

_____

_____

10. Name the most important reason that America succeeded in its revolution.

_____

Score: _____

Chapter 6 Test, Form A

The American Revolution

Matching   DIRECTIONS: Match each item in Column A with an item in Column B. Write the correct letter in each blank. *(5 points each)*

Column A

_____ 1. hired soldier

_____ 2. a plan of action

_____ 3. merchant warships

_____ 4. hit-and-run war technique

_____ 5. to leave without permission

Column B

A. mercenary

B. guerrilla warfare

C. privateers

D. desert

E. strategy

Multiple Choice   DIRECTIONS: In the blank, write the letter of the choice that best completes the statement or answers the question. *(8 points each)*

_____ 6. What was the name given to Americans who supported independence?

A. Tories

B. Separatists

C. Patriots

D. Loyalists

_____ 7. Where did the Patriot forces endure a winter of terrible suffering?

A. Valley Forge

B. Saratoga

C. Philadelphia

D. Yorktown

_____ 8. In 1780 where did the Patriots suffer their worst defeat of the war?

A. Yorktown

B. Charles Town

C. Kings Mountain

D. Trenton

_____ 9. Americans who remained loyal to Great Britain were called Loyalists or

A. Patriots.

B. Britain's Fools.

C. Tories.

D. Separatists.

_____ 10. The French nobleman who became Washington's trusted aide was

A. Francis Marion.

B. Thomas Paine.

C. the Marquis de Lafayette.

D. Benjamin Franklin.

Test, Form A (continued)

DBQ **Document-Based Questions** **DIRECTIONS:** Answer each question in the space provided. *(10 points each)*

Causes		Effects
• Long-standing hostility between Britain and France • Conflict between Britain and France during the French and Indian War • Victory at Saratoga boosts French confidence in Patriots	▶	• France lends money to the Continental Congress • France sends soldiers and ships to help American forces • Americans win independence

_____ **11.** According to the chart, which of the following did France provide to help the Americans in the Revolutionary War?

    A. money, guns, and soldiers   **C.** money and guns

    B. soldiers and food   **D.** ships, money, and soldiers

12. According to the chart, what type of relationship did the French and the British have?

_____

_____

_____

Essay **DIRECTIONS:** Answer the following question on a separate sheet of paper. *(15 points)*

13. What other nations helped the Patriots win the war? Why?

Score: _____

Chapter 6 Test, Form B

The American Revolution

Matching   DIRECTIONS: Match each item in Column A with an item in Column B. Write the correct letter in each blank. *(5 points each)*

Column A

_____ **1.** British mercenaries

_____ **2.** Swamp Fox

_____ **3.** Patriot forces

_____ **4.** taught battle tactics to the Patriots

_____ **5.** ship of John Paul Jones

Column B

A. Friedrich von Steuben

B. *Bonhomme Richard*

C. Francis Marion

D. Continental Army

E. Hessians

Multiple Choice   DIRECTIONS: In the blank, write the letter of the choice that best completes the statement or answers the question. *(8 points each)*

_____ **6.** On Christmas night 1776, the Patriots were victorious at

   A. Saratoga.
   B. Trenton.
   C. Germantown.
   D. Philadelphia.

_____ **7.** In 1777 William Howe captured what city, causing the Congress to flee?

   A. New York City
   B. Boston
   C. Washington, D.C.
   D. Philadelphia

_____ **8.** The French announced support for the United States after the American victory at

   A. Boston.
   B. Saratoga.
   C. Philadelphia.
   D. Valley Forge.

_____ **9.** George Rogers Clark forced Henry Hamilton's surrender at

   A. Fort Miami.
   B. Fort Detroit.
   C. Vincennes.
   D. Saratoga.

_____ **10.** Loyalist strength was strongest in

   A. the Ohio River valley.
   B. New York.
   C. New England.
   D. the Carolinas and Georgia.

Test, Form B (continued)

DBQ **Document-Based Questions** **DIRECTIONS:** Answer each question in the space provided. *(10 points each)*

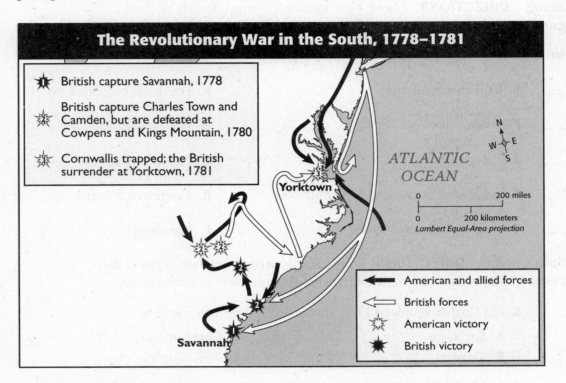

The Revolutionary War in the South, 1778–1781

☆1 British capture Savannah, 1778

☆2 British capture Charles Town and Camden, but are defeated at Cowpens and Kings Mountain, 1780

☆3 Cornwallis trapped; the British surrender at Yorktown, 1781

Yorktown

ATLANTIC OCEAN

N
W E
S

0   200 miles

0   200 kilometers
Lambert Equal-Area projection

Savannah

◄— American and allied forces

⇦ British forces

American victory

★ British victory

11. According to the map, which cities were captured by the British?

_____

_____

12. What is the last battle shown on the map?

_____

_____

Essay **DIRECTIONS:** Answer the following question on a separate sheet of paper. *(15 points)*

13. Contrast the makeup of the American and the British armies. Which differences favored the Americans?

Score: _____

Chapter 6 Test, Form C

The American Revolution

Matching   DIRECTIONS: Match each item in Column A with an item in Column B. Write the correct letter in each blank. *(5 points each)*

Column A

_____ **1.** Patriot fighter

_____ **2.** the "hair buyer"

_____ **3.** African American patriot

_____ **4.** a Polish person who contributed to the American war effort

_____ **5.** British commander of Southern forces

Column B

A. Lemuel Hayes

B. Henry Hamilton

C. Thaddeus Kosciusko

D. Margaret Corbin

E. Charles Cornwallis

Multiple Choice   DIRECTIONS: In the blank, write the letter of the choice that best completes the statement or answers the question. *(8 points each)*

_____ **6.** The militia group that defeated Burgoyne's troops at Bennington, Vermont, was called the

A. Vermont Boys.

B. Minutemen.

C. Green Mountain Boys.

D. Hessians.

_____ **7.** The British agreed to recognize the United States as an independent nation after the victory at

A. Saratoga.

B. Yorktown.

C. Vincennes.

D. New York.

_____ **8.** Which man did not represent the Americans at the peace talks in Paris?

A. George Washington

B. Benjamin Franklin

C. John Adams

D. John Jay

_____ **9.** The Hessians' main goal for winning the war was

A. land.

B. money.

C. freedom.

D. citizenship.

_____ **10.** The Americans agreed to allow British merchants to collect debts owed to them in the

A. Treaty of Great Britain.

B. Treaty of the Patriots.

C. Treaty of America.

D. Treaty of Paris.

Test, Form C (continued)

DBQ **Document-Based Questions** **DIRECTIONS:** Answer each question in the space provided. *(10 points each)*

> "Dec. 14th.— . . . The Army who have been surprisingly healthy hitherto—now begin to grow sickly from the continued fatigues they have suffered this Campaign. Yet they still show spirit of Alacrity & Contentment not to be expected from so young Troops. I am Sick—discontented—and out of humour. Poor food— hard lodging—Cold Weather—fatigue—Nasty Cloaths—nasty Cookery—. . . smoak'd out of my senses—the Devil's in't—I can't Endure it—Why are we sent here to starve and freeze—What sweet Felicities have I left at home;—A charming Wife— pretty Children—Good Beds—good food—good Cookery—all agreeable—all harmonious. Here, all Confusion—smoked Cod—hunger & filthyness—A pox on my bad luck. Here comes a bowl of beef soup—full of burnt leaves and dirt . . ."
>
> —Diary of Surgeon Albigence Waldo

_____ **11.** This account by an army surgeon at Valley Forge during the winter of 1777–1778 reveals that the Continental Army was

    A. desperate and ready to desert.

    B. enjoying the holiday season in beautiful country.

    C. terrified of sudden British attacks.

    D. surprisingly good-humored in very poor conditions.

_____ **12.** How does the army surgeon feel about this winter spent at Valley Forge?

    A. surprisingly good-humored, like the soldiers

    B. understanding and willing to endure the hardship

    C. discontented with his surroundings and longing for home

    D. proud of the troops and the army

Essay **DIRECTIONS:** Answer the following question on a separate sheet of paper. *(15 points)*

13. How did financing the war lead to inflation?

Score: _____

Section Quiz 7-1

The Articles of Confederation

Matching   **DIRECTIONS:** Match each item in Column A with an item in Column B. Write the correct letter in each blank. *(10 points each)*

Column A

_____ **1.** to give up on

_____ **2.** type of legislature established

_____ **3.** condition added to a document

_____ **4.** law

_____ **5.** a government system where the citizens rule through elected officials

Column B

A. clause

B. abandon

C. ordinance

D. republic

E. bicameral

Short Answer   **DIRECTIONS:** Answer each question below in the space provided. *(10 points each)*

6. What made Americans cautious about placing too much power in the hands of a single ruler?

_____

_____

7. Name some achievements of the Confederation government.

_____

_____

8. Which document first attempted to stop slavery in the United States?

_____

9. What plan did Robert Morris propose to help pay the national debt?

_____

_____

10. Why were the British unwilling to withdraw troops from America?

_____

_____

Score: _____

Section Quiz 7-2
Convention and Compromise

Matching   DIRECTIONS: Match each item in Column A with an item in Column B. Write the correct letter in each blank. *(10 points each)*

Column A

_____ **1.** led a rebellion

_____ **2.** supported reform of the Articles of Confederation

_____ **3.** refused to sign the Constitution without a bill of rights

_____ **4.** author of the New Jersey Plan

_____ **5.** proposed the Great Compromise

Column B

A. Elbridge Gerry

B. Roger Sherman

C. William Paterson

D. Daniel Shays

E. James Madison

Short Answer   DIRECTIONS: Answer each question below in the space provided. *(10 points each)*

6. Why did Americans want the Articles of Confederation changed?

_____

_____

7. Why did Shays's Rebellion frighten many Americans?

_____

_____

8. Who is often called the "Father of the Constitution"?

_____

9. What is a compromise?

_____

_____

10. What did George Mason propose to include in the Constitution?

_____

_____

Score: _____

Section Quiz 7-3

A New Plan of Government

Matching DIRECTIONS: Match each item in Column A with an item in Column B. Write the correct letter in each blank. *(10 points each)*

Column A

_____ **1.** supporter of the Constitution

_____ **2.** Mercy Otis Warren

_____ **3.** system that keeps any one branch of government from gaining too much power

_____ **4.** indirectly elects the president

_____ **5.** the people who shaped the Constitution

Column B

A. Antifederalist

B. Framers

C. Federalist

D. checks and balances

E. Electoral College

Short Answer DIRECTIONS: Answer each question below in the space provided. *(10 points each)*

6. Why did the Framers of the Constitution spend so much time discussing the history of political thought?

_____

_____

7. What is *federalism*?

_____

_____

8. Which branch of government can reject the appointment of judges?

_____

9. What is the purpose of the first three articles of the Constitution?

_____

_____

10. What was the strongest criticism of the Constitution?

_____

_____

Score: _____

Chapter 7 Test, Form A

A More Perfect Union

Matching   DIRECTIONS: Match each item in Column A with an item in Column B. Write the correct letter in each blank. *(5 points each)*

Column A

_____ **1.** plan of government

_____ **2.** two-house legislature

_____ **3.** to fall in value

_____ **4.** freeing of individual enslaved persons

_____ **5.** addition to a document

Column B

A. depreciate

B. amendment

C. constitution

D. manumission

E. bicameral

Multiple Choice   DIRECTIONS: In the blank, write the letter of the choice that best completes the statement or answers the question. *(8 points each)*

_____ **6.** A government in which citizens rule through elected representatives is called a

    A. monarchy.

    B. republic.

    C. theocracy.

    D. sovereignty.

_____ **7.** How many states did Congress need to pass a law under the Articles of Confederation?

    A. 3 states

    B. 7 states

    C. 9 states

    D. 13 states

_____ **8.** The division of powers between the national government and the states is a

    A. local system.

    B. feudal system.

    C. federal system.

    D. national system.

_____ **9.** What were supporters of the new Constitution called?

    A. Federalists

    B. Nationalists

    C. Antifederalists

    D. Jeffersonians

_____ **10.** A period when economic activity slows and unemployment increases is called

    A. inflation.

    B. a depression.

    C. a slowdown.

    D. a deficit.

Test, Form A (continued)

DBQ **Document-Based Questions** **DIRECTIONS:** Answer each question in the space provided. *(10 points each)*

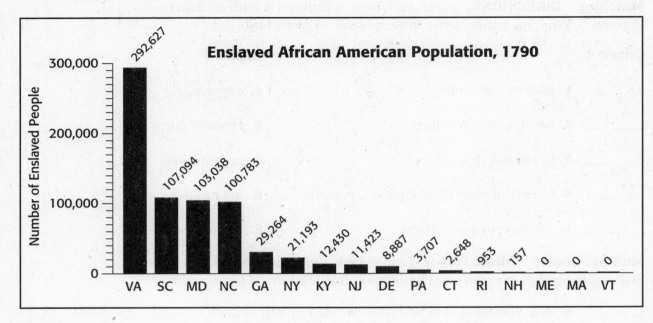

Enslaved African American Population, 1790

11. According to the bar graph, which state had the most enslaved African Americans? How many?

_____

_____

12. Other than those states with zero enslaved African Americans, which state had the fewest enslaved people? How many?

_____

_____

Essay **DIRECTIONS:** Answer the following question on a separate sheet of paper. *(15 points)*

13. What was the Three-Fifths Compromise?

Chapter 7 Test, Form B

A More Perfect Union

Matching   DIRECTIONS: Match each item in Column A with an item in Column B. Write the correct letter in each blank. *(5 points each)*

Column A

_____ 1. carries out the laws and policies of the nation

_____ 2. lawmaking branch of government

_____ 3. court system

_____ 4. created the Confederation Congress

_____ 5. created our current system of government

Column B

A. Articles of Confederation

B. legislative branch

C. Constitution

D. executive branch

E. judicial branch

Multiple Choice   DIRECTIONS: In the blank, write the letter of the choice that best completes the statement or answers the question. *(8 points each)*

_____ 6. Who suggested the Great Compromise?

    A. Roger Sherman

    B. James Madison

    C. John Adams

    D. John Locke

_____ 7. Any attempt to change the Articles of Confederation required the consent of

    A. 7 states.

    B. 13 states.

    C. 11 states.

    D. 9 states.

_____ 8. Who was the presiding officer at the Constitutional Convention?

    A. Thomas Jefferson

    B. George Washington

    C. John Adams

    D. Benjamin Franklin

_____ 9. Under the federal system, the final authority is the

    A. president.

    B. court system.

    C. Constitution.

    D. states.

_____ 10. What type of legislatures did most states establish?

    A. monarchy

    B. multihouse

    C. bicameral

    D. single-house

Test, Form B (continued)

DBQ **Document-Based Questions** **DIRECTIONS:** Answer each question in the space provided. *(10 points each)*

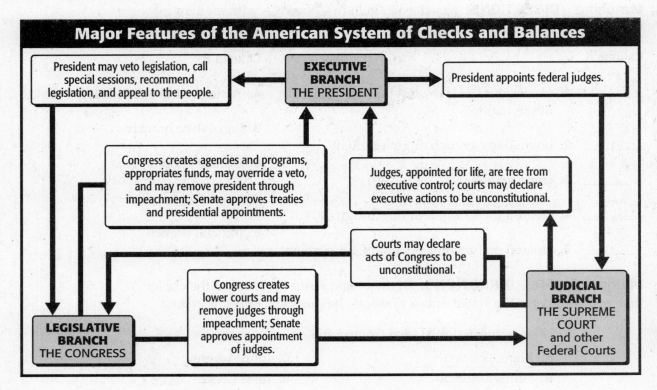

Major Features of the American System of Checks and Balances

President may veto legislation, call special sessions, recommend legislation, and appeal to the people.

EXECUTIVE BRANCH THE PRESIDENT

President appoints federal judges.

Congress creates agencies and programs, appropriates funds, may override a veto, and may remove president through impeachment; Senate approves treaties and presidential appointments.

Judges, appointed for life, are free from executive control; courts may declare executive actions to be unconstitutional.

Courts may declare acts of Congress to be unconstitutional.

LEGISLATIVE BRANCH THE CONGRESS

Congress creates lower courts and may remove judges through impeachment; Senate approves appointment of judges.

JUDICIAL BRANCH THE SUPREME COURT and other Federal Courts

_____ **11.** According to the information in the flowchart, what power does the executive branch have pertaining to legislation?

A. power to veto

C. power to impeach

B. power to appoint judges

D. power to suspend

_____ **12.** The power the legislative branch has to remove a president is called

A. veto.

C. impeachment.

B. ratification.

D. override.

Essay **DIRECTIONS:** Answer the following question on a separate sheet of paper. *(15 points)*

13. What are the three branches of government? Describe the responsibilities of each branch.

Chapter 7 Test, Form C

A More Perfect Union

Matching   DIRECTIONS: Match each item in Column A with an item in Column B. Write the correct letter in each blank. *(5 points each)*

Column A

_____ **1.** believed all people had natural rights

_____ **2.** proposed that government powers be separate and balanced

_____ **3.** introduced the Virginia Plan

_____ **4.** author of the Virginia Plan

_____ **5.** proposed the Great Compromise

Column B

A. Edmund Randolph

B. John Locke

C. James Madison

D. Roger Sherman

E. Baron de Montesquieu

Multiple Choice   DIRECTIONS: In the blank, write the letter of the choice that best completes the statement or answers the question. *(8 points each)*

_____ **6.** Which law helped stop the spread of slavery to the West?

    A. Ordinance of 1785   **C.** Northwest Ordinance

    B. Confederation Law   **D.** Morris Ordinance

_____ **7.** What keeps any one branch of government from gaining too much power?

    A. voting on a bill   **C.** vetoing

    B. the executive branch   **D.** checks and balances

_____ **8.** Which state kept its colonial charter as its constitution?

    A. Georgia   **C.** Rhode Island

    B. New York   **D.** Maryland

_____ **9.** What is the most distinctive feature of the U.S. government?

    A. federal system   **C.** executive branch

    B. separation of powers   **D.** vetoing power

_____ **10.** The president can check Congress through

    A. voting down.   **C.** overriding.

    B. lobbying.   **D.** vetoing.

Test, Form C (continued)

DBQ Document-Based Questions **DIRECTIONS:** Answer the questions in the space provided. *(10 points each)*

Article II
"Each state retains its sovereignty, freedom and independence, and every Power, Jurisdiction and right, which is not . . . expressly delegated to the United States, in Congress assembled."

Article III
"The said states hereby severally enter into a firm league of friendship with each other, for their common defense, the security of their Liberties, and their mutual and general welfare, binding themselves to assist each other, against all force offered to, or attacks made upon them, or any of them, on account of religion, sovereignty, trade, or any other pretence whatsoever."

_____ **11.** This description of the "firm league of friendship" of states is a quotation from

    A. the Constitution of the Republic.

    B. the Articles of Confederation.

    C. the Articles of Association.

    D. the Declaration of Federation.

_____ **12.** What does a "firm league of friendship" imply for the relationship of the states?

    A. States can help one another only in desperate situations.

    B. States can assist one another only when it is beneficial for both of the states involved.

    C. States must unite to protect one another for their mutual well-being.

    D. States can pick which state or states they want to help.

Essay **DIRECTIONS:** Answer the following question on a separate sheet of paper. *(15 points)*

13. What were the differences between the North and the South over the issue of slavery?

Section Quiz 8-1

The First President

Matching   DIRECTIONS: Match each item in Column A with an item in Column B. Write the correct letter in each blank. *(10 points each)*

Column A

_____ **1.** precedents

_____ **2.** first attorney general

_____ **3.** amount the government owes

_____ **4.** tax on imports

_____ **5.** first secretary of war

Column B

A. national debt

B. tariff

C. traditions

D. Henry Knox

E. Edmund Randolph

Short Answer   DIRECTIONS: Answer each question below in the space provided. *(10 points each)*

6. What is a tariff?

_____

_____

7. Within the executive branch, what did the three department heads and the attorney general come to be known as?

_____

_____

8. Who was the first leader of the new Department of State?

_____

_____

9. How did Congress establish a federal court system?

_____

_____

10. What is a speculator?

_____

_____

Score: _____

Section Quiz 8-2

Early Challenges

Matching DIRECTIONS: Match each item in Column A with an item in Column B. Write the correct letter in each blank. *(10 points each)*

Column A

_____ **1.** tax protest

_____ **2.** diplomat

_____ **3.** not taking sides

_____ **4.** force into military service

_____ **5.** agreement with Spain

Column B

A. neutrality

B. Whiskey Rebellion

C. Pinckney's Treaty

D. Edmond Genêt

E. impressment

Short Answer DIRECTIONS: Answer each question below in the space provided. *(10 points each)*

6. What was the armed protest of western Pennsylvania farmers in 1794 called? What were the farmers protesting?

_____

_____

7. Whose forces were defeated by Little Turtle in 1791?

_____

_____

8. Whose forces were defeated by Anthony Wayne in the Battle of Fallen Timbers?

_____

9. What two rights were granted by Spain with Pinckney's Treaty?

_____

_____

10. Why was Jay's Treaty unpopular?

_____

_____

Score: _____

Section Quiz 8-3

The First Political Parties

Matching   DIRECTIONS: Match each item in Column A with an item in Column B. Write the correct letter in each blank. *(10 points each)*

Column A

Column B

_____ **1.** political parties

A. Alexander Hamilton

_____ **2.** to legally overturn

B. Charles de Talleyrand

_____ **3.** French foreign minister

C. nullify

_____ **4.** Federalist

D. Thomas Jefferson

_____ **5.** Democratic-Republican

E. factions

Short Answer   DIRECTIONS: Answer each question below in the space provided. *(10 points each)*

6. Why did Washington disapprove of political parties?

_____

_____

7. Which two parties emerged by the mid-1790s?

_____

_____

8. What name did Adams give to the three French agents who demanded a bribe and a loan in 1797?

_____

9. Define the word *aliens* as it relates to this chapter in your textbook.

_____

_____

10. What did the Virginia and Kentucky Resolutions claim?

_____

_____

Score: _____

Chapter 8 Test, Form A
The Federalist Era

Matching   DIRECTIONS: Match each item in Column A with an item in Column B. Write the correct letter in each blank. *(5 points each)*

Column A

_____ **1.** first vice president

_____ **2.** favoring one side of an issue

_____ **3.** first secretary of treasury

_____ **4.** first president of the United States under the Constitution

_____ **5.** not taking sides

Column B

A. George Washington

B. Alexander Hamilton

C. John Adams

D. neutrality

E. partisan

Multiple Choice   DIRECTIONS: In the blank, write the letter of the choice that best completes the statement or answers the question. *(8 points each)*

_____ **6.** The Virginia and Kentucky Resolutions of 1798 and 1799 spelled out a theory of

    A. individual rights.   **C.** federal rights.

    B. states' rights.   **D.** soldiers' rights.

_____ **7.** Which law made it illegal to criticize the government?

    A. Alien Act   **C.** Naturalization Act

    B. Sedition Act   **D.** Tyranny Act

_____ **8.** The first 10 amendments that were added to the Constitution are called

    A. the Report on Public Credit.   **C.** the Judiciary Act of 1789.

    B. the Bill of Rights.   **D.** the American Government Plan.

_____ **9.** The amount the nation's government owes is called the

    A. national loan.   **C.** national plan.

    B. national debt.   **D.** national credit.

_____ **10.** To prepare for an election, the Federalists and the Republicans held meetings called

    A. caucuses.   **C.** political gatherings.

    B. Constitution meetings.   **D.** partisan power meetings.

Test, Form A (continued)

DBQ **Document-Based Questions**   **DIRECTIONS:** Answer the questions in the space provided. (*10 points each*)

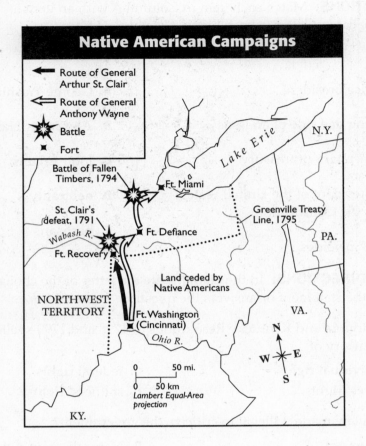

Native American Campaigns

- ← Route of General Arthur St. Clair
- ⇐ Route of General Anthony Wayne
- ✶ Battle
- ▪ Fort

Battle of Fallen Timbers, 1794
St. Clair's defeat, 1791
Wabash R.
Ft. Recovery
NORTHWEST TERRITORY
Ft. Defiance
Ft. Miami
Lake Erie
N.Y.
Greenville Treaty Line, 1795
PA.
Land ceded by Native Americans
VA.
Ft. Washington (Cincinnati)
Ohio R.
KY.

0   50 mi.
0   50 km
Lambert Equal-Area projection

_____ **11.** The map of Native American Campaigns deals with which general time period?

    A. 1780–1790   **C.** 1800–1810

    B. 1790–1800   **D.** 1760–1770

_____ **12.** According to the map, in which direction did General Anthony Wayne's forces move after they left Fort Washington?

    A. north   **C.** east

    B. south   **D.** west

Essay   **DIRECTIONS:** Answer the following question on a separate sheet of paper. (*15 points*)

13. What was the Judiciary Act of 1789?

Chapter 8 Test, Form B

The Federalist Era

Matching   DIRECTIONS: Match each item in Column A with an item in Column B. Write the correct letter in each blank. *(5 points each)*

Column A

_____ 1. leader of the Miami people

_____ 2. admired Britain

_____ 3. to legally overturn

_____ 4. deals with financial matters

_____ 5. deals with the nation's defense

Column B

A. nullify

B. Federalists

C. War Department

D. Little Turtle

E. Treasury Department

Multiple Choice   DIRECTIONS: In the blank, write the letter of the choice that best completes the statement or answers the question. *(8 points each)*

_____ 6. With which of the following did Congress establish a federal court system?

    A. Bill of Rights

    B. Hamilton's Plan

    C. Judiciary Act of 1789

    D. Report on the Public Credit

_____ 7. Which department handles relations with other nations?

    A. State Department

    B. War Department

    C. Treasury Department

    D. Foreign Department

_____ 8. To open Ohio to white settlement, Anthony Wayne forced Native American nations from the Great Lakes region to sign the

    A. Treaty of Greenville.

    B. Shawnee Treaty.

    C. Treaty of the Great Lakes.

    D. Anthony Wayne Treaty.

_____ 9. Most Americans considered Jay's Treaty

    A. dishonorable.

    B. honorable.

    C. an act of treason.

    D. an act of courage.

_____ 10. Federalists believed in

    A. free trade.

    B. state banks.

    C. a national bank.

    D. rule by the people.

Test, Form B (continued)

DBQ **Document-Based Questions** **DIRECTIONS:** Answer the questions in the space provided. *(10 points each)*

	Martha Washington	**Abigail Adams**
Life Span	born 1731, died 1802	born 1744, died 1818
First Lady	1789 to 1797	1797 to 1801
Quote	I've learned from experience that the greater part of our happiness or misery depends on our dispositions and not on our circumstances.	Learning is not attained by chance. It must be sought for with ardor and attended to with diligence.

11. How old was Abigail Adams when she became First Lady?

_____

_____

12. Who was First Lady for the shortest period of time? How many years did she spend as First Lady?

_____

_____

Essay **DIRECTIONS:** Answer the following question on a separate sheet of paper. *(15 points)*

13. Why is the Bill of Rights important?

Score: _____

Chapter 8 Test, Form C

The Federalist Era

Matching   DIRECTIONS: Match each item in Column A with an item in
Column B. Write the correct letter in each blank. *(5 points each)*

Column A

_____ 1. armed protest

_____ 2. free navigation of the Mississippi

_____ 3. did not deal with impressment

_____ 4. political meetings

_____ 5. Jefferson's running mate in 1796

Column B

A. Aaron Burr

B. Jay's Treaty

C. caucuses

D. Whiskey Rebellion

E. Pinckney's Treaty

Multiple Choice   DIRECTIONS: In the blank, write the letter of the choice
that best completes the statement or answers the question. *(8 points each)*

_____ 6. What did George Washington consider a grave danger to the
new nation?

A. the growth of political parties   **C.** France's influence

B. settlers moving west   **D.** national taxes

_____ 7. The Democratic-Republicans believed in strong state
governments and

A. rule by the wealthy class.   **C.** a strong federal government.

B. a national bank.   **D.** rule by the people.

_____ 8. Which made it more difficult for aliens to become citizens?

A. Alien Act   **C.** Naturalization Act

B. Sedition Act   **D.** XYZ affair

_____ 9. Which of the following did Thomas Jefferson support?

A. strong state government   **C.** rule by the wealthy class

B. pro-British ideas   **D.** a national bank

_____ 10. The Kentucky and Virginia Resolutions suggested that
states might

A. be bound by federal laws.   **C.** nullify federal laws.

B. write their own laws.   **D.** overturn neighboring states' laws.

Test, Form C (continued)

DBQ Document-Based Questions **DIRECTIONS:** Answer the questions in the space provided. *(10 points each)*

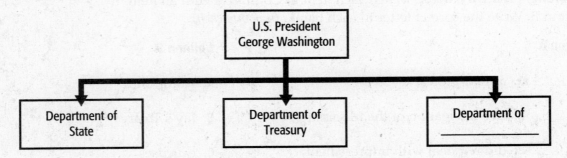

_____ **11.** The state department was established to handle

 A. relations with other nations.

 B. relations among the states.

 C. Congress.

 D. the government's legal affairs.

_____ **12.** What was the name of the third department created by Congress?

 A. Department of War

 B. Department of Defense

 C. Department of Resolution

 D. Department of Conflict

Essay **DIRECTIONS:** Answer the following question on a separate sheet of paper. *(15 points)*

13. How did the administration that took office in 1797 come to have a Federalist president and a Republican vice president?

Copyright © Glencoe/McGraw-Hill, a division of The McGraw-Hill Companies, Inc.

Score: _____

Section Quiz 9-1

The Republicans Take Power

Matching   DIRECTIONS: Match each item in Column A with an item in Column B. Write the correct letter in each blank. *(10 points each)*

Column A

_____ **1.** Thomas Jefferson's policy

_____ **2.** Jefferson's secretary of state

_____ **3.** Jefferson's secretary of the treasury

_____ **4.** Jefferson's running mate in 1800

_____ **5.** chief justice

Column B

A. James Madison

B. Aaron Burr

C. John Marshall

D. laissez-faire

E. Albert Gallatin

Short Answer   DIRECTIONS: Answer each question below in the space provided. *(10 points each)*

6. Instead of traveling around the country to gain support as in today's elections, how did the candidates in the election of 1800 campaign?

_____

_____

7. Name the candidates for president and vice president in 1800.

_____

8. How was the tie between Jefferson and Burr finally decided?

_____

_____

9. What does *laissez-faire* mean?

_____

_____

10. What did the Judiciary Act of 1801 create?

_____

_____

Name_____ Date_____ Class_____

Section Quiz 9-2

The Louisiana Purchase

Score: _____

Matching   DIRECTIONS: Match each item in Column A with an item in Column B. Write the correct letter in each blank. *(10 points each)*

Column A

_____ **1.** area west of the Mississippi River

_____ **2.** trade center

_____ **3.** France's leader

_____ **4.** revolt leader

_____ **5.** Lewis and Clark's guide

Column B

A. Toussaint-Louverture

B. Napoleon Bonaparte

C. Louisiana Territory

D. New Orleans

E. Sacagawea

Short Answer   DIRECTIONS: Answer each question below in the space provided. *(10 points each)*

6. In 1800 what country claimed the area west of the Mississippi River?

_____

_____

7. How did the Louisiana Territory come to be under French control?

_____

_____

8. For what price did the Americans agree to purchase the entire Louisiana Territory?

_____

_____

9. Why were Lewis and Clark chosen to explore the Louisiana Territory?

_____

_____

10. What political unrest did the Louisiana Purchase cause?

_____

_____

Score: _____

Section Quiz 9-3
A Time of Conflict

Matching DIRECTIONS: Match each item in Column A with an item in Column B. Write the correct letter in each blank. *(10 points each)*

Column A

_____ **1.** tribute

_____ **2.** U.S. Navy captain

_____ **3.** powerful Shawnee leader

_____ **4.** Tecumseh's brother and ally

_____ **5.** attacked Prophetstown

Column B

A. the Prophet

B. protection money

C. William Henry Harrison

D. Stephen Decatur

E. Tecumseh

Short Answer DIRECTIONS: Answer each question below in the space provided. *(10 points each)*

6. How did the war between France and Britain in the mid-1790s affect American business?

_____

_____

7. Which Barbary Coast state declared war on the United States in 1801?

_____

8. What event enraged Americans in 1807?

_____

9. Name the Shawnee chief who built a Native American confederacy.

_____

10. Which two leading War Hawks pushed for war with Britain?

_____

_____

Score: _____

Section Quiz 9-4
The War of 1812

Matching   DIRECTIONS: Match each item in Column A with an item in Column B. Write the correct letter in each blank. *(10 points each)*

Column A

_____ **1.** led Army from Detroit to Canada

_____ **2.** frigates

_____ **3.** wrote the national anthem

_____ **4.** armed private ships

_____ **5.** attacked the Creeks

Column B

A. Francis Scott Key

B. Andrew Jackson

C. privateers

D. warships

E. William Hull

Short Answer   DIRECTIONS: Answer each question below in the space provided. *(10 points each)*

6. In which month did the War of 1812 begin?

_____

7. Which naval commander seized Lake Erie from the British?

_____

_____

8. Who were the allies of the British in the War of 1812?

_____

_____

9. When the British attacked Washington, D.C., which two buildings were among those they burned?

_____

_____

10. The War of 1812 ended with what treaty?

_____

_____

Score: _____

Chapter 9 Test, Form A

The Jefferson Era

Matching DIRECTIONS: Match each item in Column A with an item in Column B. Write the correct letter in each blank. *(5 points each)*

Column A

Column B

_____ **1.** French philosophy

A. laissez-faire

_____ **2.** armed private ships

B. frigates

_____ **3.** warships

C. secede

_____ **4.** demands of Barbary pirates

D. tribute

_____ **5.** to withdraw

E. privateers

Multiple Choice DIRECTIONS: In the blank, write the letter of the choice that best completes the statement or answers the question. *(8 points each)*

_____ **6.** When the Supreme Court reviews and rules on acts of other branches of the government, it is called

    A. supremacy.

    B. law review.

    C. judicial review.

    D. Supreme ruling.

_____ **7.** Which of the following prohibited trade with other countries?

    A. Embargo Act

    B. smuggling

    C. impressment

    D. neutral rights

_____ **8.** Henry Clay and John Calhoun were known as

    A. soldiers.

    B. generals.

    C. War Hawks.

    D. peacemakers.

_____ **9.** The leaders of the exploration of the Louisiana Territory were Lewis and

    A. Adams.

    B. Burr.

    C. Pike.

    D. Clark.

_____ **10.** The British decided the war in North America was too costly after the Battle of

    A. Plattsburgh.

    B. Tippecanoe.

    C. Lake Champlain.

    D. Fort McHenry.

Test, Form A (continued)

DBQ **Document-Based Questions**   **DIRECTIONS:** Answer the questions in the space provided. *(10 points each)*

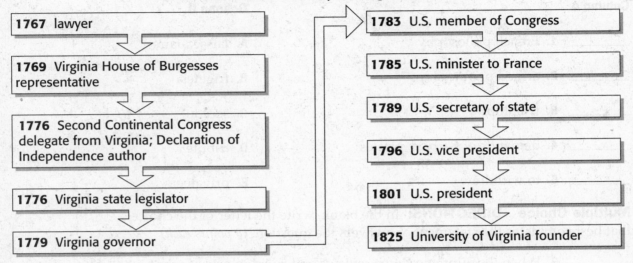

Thomas Jefferson, 1743–1826
Nicknames: "Man of the People", "Sage of Monticello"

1767 lawyer	**1783** U.S. member of Congress
1769 Virginia House of Burgesses representative	**1785** U.S. minister to France
1776 Second Continental Congress delegate from Virginia; Declaration of Independence author	**1789** U.S. secretary of state
1776 Virginia state legislator	**1796** U.S. vice president
1779 Virginia governor	**1801** U.S. president
	1825 University of Virginia founder

11. How old was Jefferson when he became a lawyer? The president?

_____

_____

12. In what year did Jefferson become president?

_____

_____

Essay   **DIRECTIONS:** Answer the following question on a separate sheet of paper. *(15 points)*

13. Who wrote "The Star-Spangled Banner" and under what conditions?

Score: _____

Chapter 9 Test, Form B

The Jefferson Era

Matching   DIRECTIONS: Match each item in Column A with an item in Column B. Write the correct letter in each blank. *(5 points each)*

Column A

Column B

_____ 1. obtained for $15 million

_____ 2. pressed for war with Great Britain

_____ 3. bans trade with another country

_____ 4. taxes on foreign imported goods

_____ 5. doubled the size of the United States

A. custom duties

B. Louisiana Territory

C. War Hawks

D. embargo

E. Louisiana Purchase

Multiple Choice   DIRECTIONS: In the blank, write the letter of the choice that best completes the statement or answers the question. *(8 points each)*

_____ 6. The election of 1800 was decided by

    A. the Senate.

    B. the House of Representatives.

    C. popular vote.

    D. the Electoral College.

_____ 7. The Louisiana Territory was purchased from

    A. Britain.

    B. France.

    C. Spain.

    D. Louisiana.

_____ 8. Who killed Alexander Hamilton in a duel in 1804?

    A. John Jay

    B. Aaron Burr

    C. Tecumseh

    D. John Adams

_____ 9. Who built a strong confederacy among Native Americans?

    A. Tecumseh

    B. Tripoli

    C. Blue Jacket

    D. the Prophet

_____ 10. Which commander destroyed the British naval forces on Lake Erie?

    A. Andrew Jackson

    B. Oliver Hazard Perry

    C. Dolley Madison

    D. William Hull

Test, Form B (continued)

DBQ **Document-Based Questions** **DIRECTIONS:** Answer the questions in the space provided. *(10 points each)*

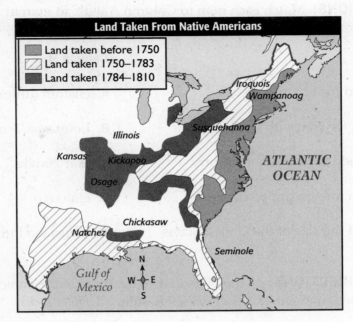

Land Taken From Native Americans

- Land taken before 1750
- Land taken 1750–1783
- Land taken 1784–1810

_____ **11.** Which people lived in present-day Florida?

    A. Creek

    B. Miami

    C. Seminole

    D. Chickasaw

_____ **12.** The Kickapoo and Osage lived on the land that was taken during which time period?

    A. land taken after 1810

    B. land taken 1784–1810

    C. land taken 1750–1783

    D. land taken before 1750

Essay **DIRECTIONS:** Answer the following question on a separate sheet of paper. *(15 points)*

13. How do today's elections differ from the election of 1800?

Name_____ Date_____ Class_____

Chapter 9 Test, Form C

The Jefferson Era

Matching DIRECTIONS: Match each item in Column A with an item in Column B. Write the correct letter in each blank. *(5 points each)*

Column A

_____ **1.** explored with Lewis and Clark

_____ **2.** burned the *Philadelphia*

_____ **3.** set up regional courts

_____ **4.** lost the public's respect

_____ **5.** took over the Republican Party

Column B

A. York

B. Federalists

C. War Hawks

D. Stephen Decatur

E. Judiciary Act of 1801

Multiple Choice DIRECTIONS: In the blank, write the letter of the choice that best completes the statement or answers the question. *(8 points each)*

_____ **6.** The size of the United States doubled with

    A. the adoption of New Orleans.

    B. Zebulon Pike's expedition.

    C. the expedition of Lewis and Clark.

    D. the Louisiana Purchase.

_____ **7.** Who forced Napoleon Bonaparte to abandon plans for an American empire?

    A. Toussaint-Louverture

    B. Zebulon Pike

    C. Aaron Burr

    D. Meriwether Lewis

_____ **8.** Who urged Native Americans to return to the customs of their ancestors?

    A. Tecumseh

    B. Blue Jacket

    C. the Prophet

    D. Tippecanoe

_____ **9.** Requirements for presidential elections were set by the

    A. Tenth Amendment.

    B. Thirteenth Amendment.

    C. Fifteenth Amendment.

    D. Twelfth Amendment.

_____ **10.** Hopes for a Native American confederation disappeared with the death of

    A. the Prophet.

    B. Tripoli.

    C. Tecumseh.

    D. Blue Jacket.

Test, Form C (continued)

DBQ **Document-Based Questions** **DIRECTIONS:** Answer the questions in the space provided. *(10 points each)*

Thomas Jefferson, 1743–1826
Nicknames: "Man of the People", "Sage of Monticello"

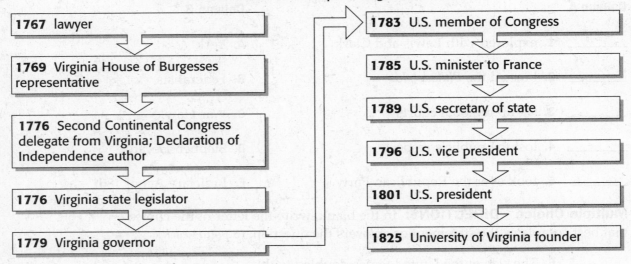

1767 lawyer	**1783** U.S. member of Congress
1769 Virginia House of Burgesses representative	**1785** U.S. minister to France
1776 Second Continental Congress delegate from Virginia; Declaration of Independence author	**1789** U.S. secretary of state
1776 Virginia state legislator	**1796** U.S. vice president
1779 Virginia governor	**1801** U.S. president
	1825 University of Virginia founder

11. What do you think the nickname "Man of the People" meant?

_____

_____

12. What position did Jefferson hold when he was 46 years old?

_____

_____

Essay **DIRECTIONS:** Answer the following question on a separate sheet of paper. *(15 points)*

13. What are the three principles of judicial review established by the *Marbury* v. *Madison* decision?

Score: _____

Section Quiz 10-1
Economic Growth

Matching **DIRECTIONS:** Match each item in Column A with an item in Column B. Write the correct letter in each blank. *(10 points each)*

Column A

_____ **1.** money for investment

_____ **2.** shares of ownership in a company

_____ **3.** invented cotton gin

_____ **4.** launched factory system in United States

_____ **5.** factory workers

Column B

A. stock

B. Francis Cabot Lowell

C. capital

D. Lowell girls

E. Eli Whitney

Short Answer **DIRECTIONS:** Answer each question below in the space provided. *(10 points each)*

6. When did the Industrial Revolution take root in the United States?

_____

7. How did Samuel Slater introduce cotton manufacturing in Rhode Island?

_____

_____

8. Which economic system invests money in businesses in hopes of making a profit?

_____

_____

9. What three factors encouraged people to invest in new industries?

_____

_____

10. What is a patent?

_____

_____

Score: _____

Section Quiz 10-2
Westward Bound

Matching   DIRECTIONS: Match each item in Column A with an item in Column B. Write the correct letter in each blank. *(10 points each)*

Column A

_____ **1.** official count of the population

_____ **2.** toll roads

_____ **3.** designed the *Clermont*

_____ **4.** planned the Erie Canal

_____ **5.** artificial waterway

Column B

A. canal

B. Robert Fulton

C. turnpikes

D. census

E. De Witt Clinton

Short Answer   DIRECTIONS: Answer each question below in the space provided. *(10 points each)*

6. What was the population when the first census was taken?

_____

_____

7. What was the opinion of Congress about the National Road?

_____

_____

8. How long did it take the *Clermont* to make the 150-mile trip from New York City to Albany? How long was the trip using only sails?

_____

_____

9. How did boats and barges navigate the Erie Canal in the years before steamboats were allowed?

_____

_____

10. How many new states were admitted to the union between 1791 and 1821?

_____

Section Quiz 10-3
Unity and Sectionalism

Matching   DIRECTIONS: Match each item in Column A with an item in Column B. Write the correct letter in each blank. *(10 points each)*

Column A

Column B

_____ **1.** loyalty to a region

A. John C. Calhoun

_____ **2.** internal improvements

B. sectionalism

_____ **3.** advocate of states' rights

C. Daniel Webster

_____ **4.** spoke against sectionalism

D. Henry Clay

_____ **5.** negotiated the Treaty of Ghent

E. federal projects

Short Answer   DIRECTIONS: Answer each question below in the space provided. *(10 points each)*

6. What helped forge a sense of national unity after the War of 1812?

_____

_____

7. What is state sovereignty?

_____

_____

8. What was the nickname given to Henry Clay?

_____

_____

9. Which European country claimed ownership of Florida?

_____

_____

10. What action did the Monroe Doctrine forbid?

_____

_____

Score: _____

Chapter 10 Test, Form A
Growth and Expansion

Matching   DIRECTIONS: Match each item in Column A with an item in Column B. Write the correct letter in each blank. *(5 points each)*

Column A

_____ 1. gives legal rights to inventions

_____ 2. autonomous power

_____ 3. toll road

_____ 4. loyalty to a region

_____ 5. artificial waterway

Column B

A. sectionalism

B. sovereignty

C. canal

D. patent

E. turnpike

Multiple Choice   DIRECTIONS: In the blank, write the letter of the choice that best completes the statement or answers the question. *(8 points each)*

_____ 6. Who invented the cotton gin?

    A. Samuel Slater   **C.** Eli Whitney

    B. James Rumsey   **D.** Francis Cabot Lowell

_____ 7. The _____ changed the way people worked.

    A. Technology Revolution   **C.** Industrial Revolution

    B. Modern Revolution   **D.** Machinery Revolution

_____ 8. All manufacturing steps are brought together in one place under

    A. a corporation.   **C.** the factory system.

    B. free enterprise.   **D.** a contract.

_____ 9. Separate canal compartments where water levels are raised or lowered are called

    A. canals.   **C.** turnpikes.

    B. locks.   **D.** shelves.

_____ 10. Named after a cloth, roads consisting of logs laid side by side are called

    A. ridge roads.   **C.** cotton roads.

    B. corduroy roads.   **D.** silk roads.

Test, Form A (continued)

 Document-Based Questions   **DIRECTIONS:** Answer the questions
in the space provided. *(10 points each)*

Henry Clay's American System

The policy would have enforced a protective tariff to get funding for transportation improvements.

↓

These improvements would be the construction of better roads and canals.

↓

This would allow industrialization to prosper because the raw materials of the South and the West could easily and inexpensively get into the North and the East for manufacturing.

↓

The manufactured goods could then be shipped back to the South and the West.

11. What were the two improvements that Clay intended his tariffs to
support?

_____

_____

12. Once the improvements were made to roads and canals, what did Clay
foresee happening?

_____

_____

Essay   DIRECTIONS: Answer the following question on a separate sheet
of paper. *(15 points)*

13. What is sectionalism and how did it hurt the United States?

Score: _____

Chapter 10 Test, Form B

Growth and Expansion

Matching   DIRECTIONS: Match each item in Column A with an item in Column B. Write the correct letter in each blank. *(5 points each)*

Column A

_____ 1. changed how people worked

_____ 2. population count

_____ 3. money for investment

_____ 4. uniform pieces

_____ 5. developed by Robert Fulton

Column B

A. steamboat

B. Industrial Revolution

C. census

D. interchangeable parts

E. capital

Multiple Choice   DIRECTIONS: In the blank, write the letter of the choice that best completes the statement or answers the question. *(8 points each)*

_____ 6. Changes in the way goods were made in the mid-1700s began in

    A. France.
    B. Spain.
    C. Britain.
    D. the United States.

_____ 7. America's Industrial Revolution began to take root in

    A. New England.
    B. the West.
    C. the Middle Atlantic.
    D. the South.

_____ 8. The National Road went as far west as

    A. Vandalia, Ohio.
    B. Cincinnati, Ohio.
    C. Vandalia, Illinois.
    D. Indianapolis, Indiana.

_____ 9. Which of the following called for a tariff to stimulate growth of American industries?

    A. American System
    B. Embargo Act
    C. urban growth
    D. National Bank

_____ 10. Which agreement set the official border between Canada and the United States?

    A. Rush-Bagot Treaty
    B. Monroe Doctrine
    C. Adams-Onís Treaty
    D. Convention of 1818

Test, Form B (continued)

DBQ **Document-Based Questions** **DIRECTIONS:** Answer the questions in the space provided. *(10 points each)*

> " . . . Of events in that quarter of the globe, with which we have so much [connection] and from which we derive our origin, we have always been anxious and interested spectators. The citizens of the United States cherish sentiments the most friendly in favor of the liberty and happiness of their fellow-men on that side of the Atlantic. In the wars of the European powers in matters relating to themselves we have never taken any part, nor does it comport with our policy so to do. It is only when our rights are invaded or seriously menaced that we resent injuries or make preparation for our defense. . . ."
>
> —December 2, 1823

_____ **11.** This discussion of U.S. foreign policy is a quotation from the

     A. Treaty of Ghent.   **C.** Monroe Doctrine.

     B. Missouri Compromise.   **D.** Rush-Bagot Treaty.

_____ **12.** Which "quarter of the globe" is being addressed in this quote?

     A. Great Britain   **C.** Asia

     B. Germany   **D.** Europe

Essay **DIRECTIONS:** Answer the following question on a separate sheet of paper. *(15 points)*

13. Which inventions of the early 1800s made the Industrial Revolution possible?

Score: _____

Chapter 10 Test, Form C
Growth and Expansion

Matching DIRECTIONS: Match each item in Column A with an item in Column B. Write the correct letter in each blank. *(5 points each)*

Column A

_____ **1.** James Monroe's secretary of state

_____ **2.** invaded Spanish East Florida in 1818

_____ **3.** favored the Tariff of 1816

_____ **4.** Mexican revolutionary

_____ **5.** negotiated by Henry Clay

Column B

A. Andrew Jackson

B. Miguel Hidalgo

C. Missouri Compromise

D. John Quincy Adams

E. Daniel Webster

Multiple Choice DIRECTIONS: In the blank, write the letter of the choice that best completes the statement or answers the question. *(8 points each)*

_____ **6.** Pioneer families tended to settle in communities
    A. far from others.
    B. near the sea.
    C. along the rivers.
    D. on railroads.

_____ **7.** An example of U.S. "military strength" was the
    A. Adams-Onís Treaty.
    B. Monroe Doctrine.
    C. Convention of 1818.
    D. Rush-Bagot Treaty.

_____ **8.** Thirty years after the first census, the population of the United States was
    A. 4 million.
    B. 7 million.
    C. 2 million.
    D. 10 million.

_____ **9.** Which document became an important part of American foreign policy in 1823?
    A. Monroe Doctrine
    B. Missouri Compromise
    C. Adams-Onís Treaty
    D. Rush-Bagot Treaty

_____ **10.** The period of national harmony ended because of
    A. regional differences.
    B. political parties.
    C. arguments over the flag.
    D. arguments over war.

Test, Form C (continued)

 Document-Based Questions   **DIRECTIONS:** Answer the questions in the space provided. *(10 points each)*

Henry Clay's American System

> The policy would have enforced a protective tariff to get funding for transportation improvements.

> These improvements would be the construction of better roads and canals.

> This would allow industrialization to prosper because the raw materials of the South and the West could easily and inexpensively get into the North and the East for manufacturing.

> The manufactured goods could then be shipped back to the South and the West.

11. Why do you think Clay called the plan the "American System"?

_____

_____

12. How was Clay's proposal supposed to benefit the entire country?

_____

_____

Essay   DIRECTIONS: Answer the following question on a separate sheet of paper. *(15 points)*

13. What factors do you think contributed to President James Monroe's reelection?

Score: _____

Section Quiz 11-1

Jacksonian Democracy

Matching   DIRECTIONS: Match each item in Column A with an item in Column B. Write the correct letter in each blank. *(10 points each)*

Column A

_____ 1. deal between Clay and Adams in the election of 1824

_____ 2. favored states' rights in 1828

_____ 3. largest single share

_____ 4. small farmers, craft workers, and the poor

_____ 5. insults in the election of 1828

Column B

A. Democratic-Republicans

B. mudslinging

C. Jackson's supporters

D. plurality

E. the "corrupt bargain"

Short Answer   DIRECTIONS: Answer each question below in the space provided. *(10 points each)*

6. In the 1828 election, which political party supported a strong central government and backed John Quincy Adams?

_____

7. What is the term for the practice of replacing government employees with the winning candidate's supporters?

_____

8. During Jackson's tenure in office, the Congress-controlled caucuses were replaced with a more democratic system called what?

_____

9. What is another name for taxes on imports that became a controversial issue between Jackson and Southern states?

_____

10. In response to South Carolina's Nullification Act, what bill did Congress pass that allowed military action to enforce acts of Congress?

_____

Score: _____

Section Quiz 11-2
Conflicts Over Land

Matching   DIRECTIONS: Match each item in Column A with an item in Column B. Write the correct letter in each blank. *(10 points each)*

Column A

_____ 1. Osceola

_____ 2. Black Hawk

_____ 3. Winfield Scott

_____ 4. invented Cherokee alphabet

_____ 5. refused to recognize Cherokee laws

Column B

A. led Sauk and Fox warriors

B. Sequoyah

C. sent to remove the Cherokee

D. Georgia

E. led Seminole rebellion

Short Answer   DIRECTIONS: Answer each question below in the space provided. *(10 points each)*

6. Which act, passed by Congress in 1830, authorized the federal government to pay Native Americans to move west?

_____

7. Which Native American nation pursued its case against relocation to the Supreme Court in the case *Worcester* v. *Georgia*?

_____

8. What did Osceola and some of his people do when they were pressured to leave Florida in the 1830s?

_____

_____

9. What do historians call the forced removal of the Cherokee from their native lands to present-day Oklahoma?

_____

10. Which Native Americans participated in the Dade Massacre so they could remain on their lands?

_____

Score: _____

Section Quiz 11-3
Jackson and the Bank

Matching   DIRECTIONS: Match each item in Column A with an item in Column B. Write the correct letter in each blank. *(10 points each)*

Column A

_____ 1. Van Buren's policy toward the economy

_____ 2. Whig who used to be a Democrat

_____ 3. began with the Panic of 1837

_____ 4. supported Jackson's veto of the bank charter bill

_____ 5. Tippecanoe

Column B

A. John Tyler

B. depression

C. the voters in 1832

D. laissez-faire

E. William Henry Harrison

Short Answer   DIRECTIONS: Answer each question below in the space provided. *(10 points each)*

6. Who was the president of the Bank of the United States and a person that President Jackson disliked?

_____

7. Which Supreme Court decision found the Bank of the United States to be legal under the U.S. Constitution?

_____

8. How did President Jackson finally "kill" the Bank of the United States?

_____

_____

9. Name three negative consequences of the Panic of 1837.

_____

_____

10. What did President Van Buren establish to handle the government's money?

_____

_____

Score: _____

Chapter 11 Test, Form A
The Jackson Era

Matching   DIRECTIONS: Match each item in Column A with an item in Column B. Write the correct letter in each blank. *(5 points each)*

Column A

_____ **1.** an overwhelming victory

_____ **2.** the process of moving to a new place

_____ **3.** largest single share

_____ **4.** more than half

_____ **5.** to cancel

Column B

A. relocation

B. majority

C. nullify

D. landslide

E. plurality

Multiple Choice   DIRECTIONS: In the blank, write the letter of the choice that best completes the statement or answers the question. *(8 points each)*

_____ **6.** Which president's popularity with the "common man" changed politics?

    A. Martin Van Buren   **C.** John Quincy Adams

    B. Andrew Jackson   **D.** William Henry Harrison

_____ **7.** Some Southerners wanted to break away from the United States, or to

    A. nullify.   **C.** secede.

    B. caucus.   **D.** expand.

_____ **8.** Who won the 1824 presidential election?

    A. Andrew Jackson   **C.** William H. Crawford

    B. John Quincy Adams   **D.** Henry Clay

_____ **9.** The practice of replacing government employees with the winning candidate's supporters became known as

    A. mudslinging.   **C.** bureaucracy.

    B. the spoils system.   **D.** suffrage.

_____ **10.** A government permit to operate the Bank of the United States was called a

    A. charter.   **C.** bureaucracy.

    B. bank permit.   **D.** bank loan.

Test, Form A (continued)

DBQ **Document-Based Questions** **DIRECTIONS:** Answer the questions in the space provided. *(10 points each)*

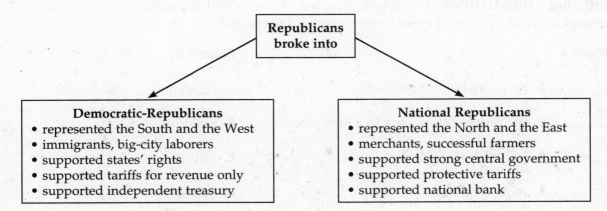

11. In which regions did most new National Republicans live?

_____

12. In which regions did most Democratic-Republicans live?

_____

Essay **DIRECTIONS:** Answer the following question on a separate sheet of paper. *(15 points)*

13. What was the "corrupt bargain" between Henry Clay and John Quincy Adams?

Score: _____

Chapter 11 Test, Form B

The Jackson Era

Matching   DIRECTIONS: Match each item in Column A with an item in Column B. Write the correct letter in each blank. *(5 points each)*

Column A

_____ **1.** Andrew Jackson's opponent in 1828

_____ **2.** mistrusted strong central government

_____ **3.** wanted strong central government

_____ **4.** opposed Jackson on issues about the National Bank

_____ **5.** Andrew Jackson's rivals

Column B

A. National Republicans

B. Whigs

C. Democratic-Republicans

D. John Quincy Adams

E. Henry Clay

Multiple Choice   DIRECTIONS: In the blank, write the letter of the choice that best completes the statement or answers the question. *(8 points each)*

_____ **6.** Which 1824 presidential nominee was the son of a former president?

　A. Henry Clay

　B. Andrew Jackson

　C. John Quincy Adams

　D. William H. Crawford

_____ **7.** Which act did Congress pass in order to relocate Native Americans?

　A. Naturalization Act

　B. Alien Act

　C. Relocation Act

　D. Indian Removal Act

_____ **8.** The Bank of the United States was chartered by

　A. merchants.

　B. the president.

　C. Congress.

　D. Republicans.

_____ **9.** Which president was raised in poverty?

　A. John Quincy Adams

　B. Martin Van Buren

　C. Andrew Jackson

　D. Henry Clay

_____ **10.** Which of the following showed that the federal government would not allow a state to go its own way without a fight?

　A. suffrage

　B. bureaucracy

　C. Force Bill

　D. spoils system

Test, Form B (continued)

DBQ **Document-Based Questions** **DIRECTIONS:** Answer the questions in the space provided. *(10 points each)*

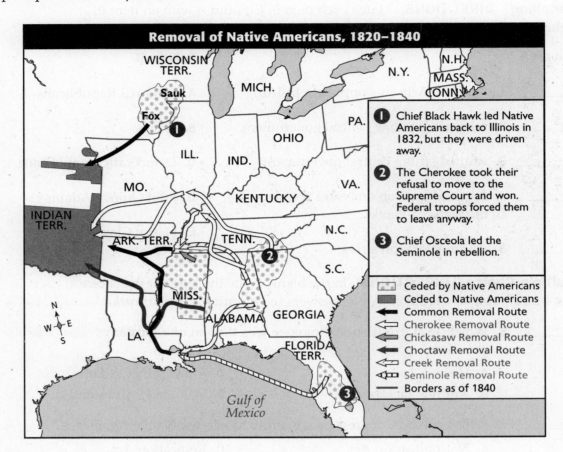

Removal of Native Americans, 1820–1840

_____ **11.** According to the information on the map, who tried to lead his people back to their native land in Illinois in 1832?

    A. Spotted Eagle   **C.** Chief Joseph

    B. Chief Black Hawk   **D.** Chief Red Cloud

_____ **12.** Which people were forcibly removed from their native land in Florida?

    A. Walla Walla   **C.** Cherokee

    B. Choctaw   **D.** Seminole

Essay **DIRECTIONS:** Answer the following question on a separate sheet of paper. *(15 points)*

13. Summarize the Supreme Court case of *Worcester* v. *Georgia.*

Score: _____

Chapter 11 Test, Form C

The Jackson Era

Matching   **DIRECTIONS:** Match each item in Column A with an item in Column B. Write the correct letter in each blank. *(5 points each)*

Column A

_____ **1.** 1828 Democratic-Republican candidate

_____ **2.** inaugurated in 1837

_____ **3.** defended nullification

_____ **4.** 1844 Democratic candidate

_____ **5.** 1840 Whig candidate

Column B

A. James Polk

B. John C. Calhoun

C. Andrew Jackson

D. William Henry Harrison

E. Martin Van Buren

Multiple Choice   **DIRECTIONS:** In the blank, write the letter of the choice that best completes the statement or answers the question. *(8 points each)*

_____ **6.** The 1824 presidential election was decided

    A. in the House of Representatives.

    B. by the Electoral College.

    C. by popular vote.

    D. by the political parties.

_____ **7.** Which candidate for president in 1824 was Speaker of the House of Representatives?

    A. Martin Van Buren

    B. Henry Clay

    C. Andrew Jackson

    D. John Quincy Adams

_____ **8.** John Tyler became president because

    A. of the popular vote.

    B. he was appointed.

    C. President Harrison had died.

    D. he was elected.

_____ **9.** Which person was a favorite son candidate from Tennessee in the 1824 election?

    A. Henry Clay

    B. Andrew Jackson

    C. John Quincy Adams

    D. William H. Crawford

_____ **10.** To win the election of 1840, William Henry Harrison needed the support of

    A. landowners.

    B. bankers.

    C. laborers.

    D. Congress.

Test, Form C (continued)

DBQ **Document-Based Questions** **DIRECTIONS:** Answer the questions in the space provided. *(10 points each)*

> "On Tuesday evening we fell in with a detachment of the poor Cherokee Indians . . . about eleven hundred Indians . . . We found them in the forest camped for the night by the road side. . . . under a severe fall of rain accompanied by heavy wind. With their canvas for a shield from the inclemency of the weather, and the cold wet ground for a resting place, after the fatigue of the day, they spent the night . . . many of the aged Indians were suffering extremely from the fatigue of the journey . . . several were then quite ill and one aged man we were informed was then in the last struggles of death."
>
> —Newspaper account of Cherokee removal

_____ **11.** An estimated 4,000 Cherokee died during this removal known to the Cherokee people as

    A. Trail of Sadness.   **C.** Trail of Death.

    B. Trail Where They Cried.   **D.** Trail of Tears.

_____ **12.** The word that *best* describes the attitude of the writer of this passage is

    A. detached.   **C.** sympathetic.

    B. curious.   **D.** hostile.

Essay **DIRECTIONS:** Answer the following question on a separate sheet of paper. *(15 points)*

13. How did the 1828 tariff create a struggle between the North and the South?

Section Quiz 12-1

The Oregon Country

Matching   DIRECTIONS: Match each item in Column A with an item in Column B. Write the correct letter in each blank. *(10 points each)*

Column A

_____ **1.** American merchant

_____ **2.** fur trappers

_____ **3.** rendezvous

_____ **4.** missionary

_____ **5.** national mission of expansion

Column B

A. mountain men

B. meeting

C. Dr. Marcus Whitman

D. Manifest Destiny

E. John Jacob Astor

Short Answer   DIRECTIONS: Answer each question below in the space provided. *(10 points each)*

6. In order to gain rights to the Oregon country, the United States had to negotiate with which three countries?

_____

_____

7. Who were the first Americans to reach the Oregon country?

_____

8. Which Native American people did Dr. Marcus Whitman build a mission among?

_____

_____

9. In which state did the Oregon Trail originate?

_____

10. To what did the Democratic slogan "Fifty-Four Forty or Fight" refer?

_____

_____

Score: _____

Section Quiz 12-2
Independence for Texas

Matching   DIRECTIONS: Match each item in Column A with an item in Column B. Write the correct letter in each blank. *(10 points each)*

Column A

_____ **1.** empresario

_____ **2.** recruited 300 families to settle in Texas

_____ **3.** official order

_____ **4.** Mexican dictator

_____ **5.** Alamo commander

Column B

A. Stephen F. Austin

B. William B. Travis

C. Moses Austin

D. General Antonio López de Santa Anna

E. decree

Short Answer   DIRECTIONS: Answer each question below in the space provided. *(10 points each)*

6. What four promises did colonists have to make in exchange for Mexican land at extremely low prices?

_____

_____

7. What were *empresarios*?

_____

_____

8. In 1830 what decree from the Mexican government angered Texans?

_____

9. How long did the battle of the Alamo last?

_____

10. Why did President Andrew Jackson refuse Houston's request to annex Texas?

_____

_____

Score: _____

Section Quiz 12-3
War With Mexico

Matching   DIRECTIONS: Match each item in Column A with an item in
Column B. Write the correct letter in each blank. *(10 points each)*

Column A

_____ **1.** plotted war with Mexico

_____ **2.** mission slaves

_____ **3.** ranch owners

_____ **4.** Republic of California

_____ **5.** captured Mexico City

Column B

A. Native Americans

B. Bear Flag Republic

C. President Polk

D. Winfield Scott

E. rancheros

Short Answer   DIRECTIONS: Answer each question below in the space
provided. *(10 points each)*

6. What did William Becknell's trading route come to be known as?

_____

7. What did Americans argue would be two advantages of adding
California to the Union?

_____

_____

8. How much was John Slidell authorized to offer Mexico for California
and New Mexico and for accepting the Rio Grande as the Texas border?

_____

9. Who were the Californios?

_____

_____

10. What did the Treaty of Guadalupe Hidalgo establish?

_____

_____

Score: _____

Section Quiz 12-4
California and Utah

Matching   DIRECTIONS: Match each item in Column A with an item in Column B. Write the correct letter in each blank. *(10 points each)*

Column A

_____ **1.** gold seekers

_____ **2.** Gold Rush communities

_____ **3.** sold denim pants to miners

_____ **4.** members of vigilance committees for security

_____ **5.** settled near the Great Salt Lake in Utah

Column B

A. boomtowns

B. Levi Strauss

C. Mormons

D. forty-niners

E. vigilantes

Short Answer   DIRECTIONS: Answer each question below in the space provided. *(10 points each)*

6. What did the Land Law of 1851 establish?

_____

_____

7. Who was Brigham Young?

_____

_____

8. When did California write a constitution and apply for statehood?

_____

9. From where did Joseph Smith say he received the ideas for *The Book of Mormon*?

_____

_____

10. What was the largest single migration in American history?

_____

_____

Score: _____

Chapter 12 Test, Form A

Manifest Destiny

Matching   DIRECTIONS: Match each item in Column A with an item in Column B. Write the correct letter in each blank. *(5 points each)*

Column A

_____ **1.** took the law into their own hands

_____ **2.** official order

_____ **3.** gold seekers

_____ **4.** huge Mexican properties

_____ **5.** a meeting

Column B

A. ranchos

B. rendezvous

C. forty-niners

D. vigilantes

E. decree

Multiple Choice   DIRECTIONS: In the blank, write the letter of the choice that best completes the statement or answers the question. *(8 points each)*

_____ **6.** Mountain men made their living as

    A. merchants.   **C.** politicians.

    B. teachers.   **D.** fur trappers.

_____ **7.** Founded by the Mormons, which city was originally called Deseret?

    A. San Diego   **C.** Santa Fe

    B. Provo   **D.** Salt Lake City

_____ **8.** Oregon country was which direction from California?

    A. north   **C.** east

    B. south   **D.** west

_____ **9.** Reports of what persuaded many Americans to settle in Oregon country?

    A. gold   **C.** free land

    B. fertile land   **D.** religious freedom

_____ **10.** What did the United States insist was the border between the United States and Mexico?

    A. Rio Grande   **C.** the Alamo

    B. Nueces River   **D.** Mexico City

Test, Form A (continued)

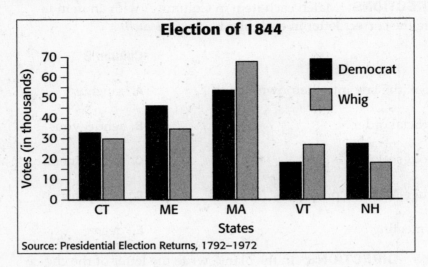

DBQ Document-Based Questions **DIRECTIONS:** Answer the questions in the space provided. *(10 points each)*

Election of 1844

Votes (in thousands)

- ■ Democrat
- ▨ Whig

States: CT, ME, MA, VT, NH

Source: Presidential Election Returns, 1792–1972

11. Who won more states, Democrats or Whigs?

_____

_____

12. In which state did the Whigs receive the most votes?

_____

_____

Essay   DIRECTIONS: Answer the following question on a separate sheet of paper. *(15 points)*

13. Who were the forty-niners, and why did they come to California?

Chapter 12 Test, Form B
Manifest Destiny

Matching   DIRECTIONS: Match each item in Column A with an item in Column B. Write the correct letter in each blank. *(5 points each)*

Column A

_____ **1.** Green River explorer

_____ **2.** army officer who sparked interest in California

_____ **3.** brought measles epidemic to Cayuse by accident

_____ **4.** first American trader to reach Santa Fe

_____ **5.** brought first American settlers to Texas

Column B

A. Jim Beckwourth

B. William Becknell

C. John C. Frémont

D. Stephen Austin

E. Marcus Whitman

Multiple Choice   DIRECTIONS: In the blank, write the letter of the choice that best completes the statement or answers the question. *(8 points each)*

_____ **6.** Which was the last country to challenge U.S. control of Oregon?

A. Russia

B. Britain

C. Spain

D. Mexico

_____ **7.** Which of the following allowed people from both Britain and the United States to settle in Oregon country?

A. joint occupation

B. rendezvous

C. Manifest Destiny

D. Oregon country occupation

_____ **8.** Commander in chief of the Texas forces was

A. William B. Travis.

B. Sam Houston.

C. Stephen F. Austin.

D. Jim Bowie.

_____ **9.** Which people made huge profits during the Gold Rush?

A. merchants

B. teachers

C. miners

D. missionaries

_____ **10.** Who led the Mormon migration to the Great Salt Lake area?

A. Joseph Smith

B. John Sutter

C. Levi Strauss

D. Brigham Young

Test, Form B (continued)

DBQ Document-Based Questions **DIRECTIONS:** Answer the questions in the space provided. *(10 points each)*

> "It is time now for opposition to the annexation of Texas to cease, . . .
>
> "Other nations have undertaken to intrude themselves into it, between us and the proper parties to the case, in a spirit of hostile interference against us, for the avowed object of thwarting our policy and hampering our power, limiting our greatness and checking the fulfillment of our manifest destiny to overspread the continent allotted by Providence for the free development of our yearly multiplying millions. . . ."
>
> —John L. O'Sullivan, *United States Magazine and Democratic Review,* July 1845

_____ 11. In this passage, O'Sullivan describes "manifest destiny" as the right of

    A. Texas to become part of the United States.

    B. the United States to expand its territory across North America.

    C. other nations to oppose the actions of the United States.

    D. New Mexico and California to become independent republics.

_____ 12. What does the phrase "continent allotted by Providence" mean?

    A. land chosen by God   **C.** land for Catholics only

    B. land taken from Rhode Island   **D.** land destined for greatness

Essay DIRECTIONS: Answer the following question on a separate sheet of paper. *(15 points)*

13. How did President James K. Polk get Americans to go to war with Mexico?

Score: _____

Chapter 12 Test, Form C
Manifest Destiny

Matching   **DIRECTIONS:** Match each item in Column A with an item in Column B. Write the correct letter in each blank. *(5 points each)*

Column A

Column B

_____ 1. way to Oregon country

A. Kit Carson

_____ 2. William Becknell's route

B. Deseret

_____ 3. mountain man turned guide

C. Antonio López de Santa Anna

_____ 4. ordered Texans' execution

D. Santa Fe Trail

_____ 5. Mormon land in Utah

E. Oregon Trail

Multiple Choice   **DIRECTIONS:** In the blank, write the letter of the choice that best completes the statement or answers the question. *(8 points each)*

_____ 6. During the siege at the Alamo, Texan leaders were

   A. meeting with U.S. officials.

   B. bringing more ammunition from San Antonio.

   C. writing a new constitution.

   D. negotiating annexation terms.

_____ 7. The third part of James K. Polk's war plan was to

   A. capture Mexico City.

   B. seize California.

   C. drive Mexicans out of borderlands.

   D. seize New Mexico.

_____ 8. Which was the high point of the year for mountain men?

   A. trading merchandise

   B. Native American parties

   C. the rendezvous

   D. meeting settlers

_____ 9. Which town in California was seized by a small group and renamed the Bear Flag Republic?

   A. San Francisco

   B. San Diego

   C. Buena Vista

   D. Sonoma

_____ 10. Which event ended in a few years but had long-lasting effects on California's economy?

   A. Gold Rush

   B. shipping

   C. agriculture

   D. trade

Name_____ Date_____ Class_____

DBQ **Document-Based Questions** **DIRECTIONS:** Answer the questions
in the space provided. *(10 points each)*

> "We reached the camping place. What first struck our eye was several long rows of Indian tents (lodges), extending along the Green River for at least a mile. Indians and whites were mingled here in varied groups. Of the Indians there had come chiefly Snakes, Flatheads and Nezperces, peaceful tribes, living beyond the Rocky Mountains. Of whites the agents of the different trading companies and a quantity of trappers had found their way here, visiting this fair of the wilderness to buy and to sell, to renew old contracts and to make new ones, to make arrangements for future meetings, to meet old friends, to tell of adventures they had been through, and to spend for once a jolly day."
> —Adolph Wislizenus, a German traveler in the West

_____ 11. Who came to this meeting of mountain men?

   A. agents of trading companies, settlers, soldiers

   B. Native Americans, agents of trading companies, trappers

   C. trappers, church leaders, Native Americans

   D. settlers, soldiers, trappers, agents of trading companies

12. Considering what you know of American history up to this time, what is unique about Wislizenus's observations?

_____

_____

Essay **DIRECTIONS:** Answer the following question on a separate sheet of paper. *(15 points)*

13. How did the early settlers of the West help pave the way for the California Gold Rush?

Score: _____

Section Quiz 13-1

The North's Economy

Matching   DIRECTIONS: Match each item in Column A with an item in Column B. Write the correct letter in each blank. *(10 points each)*

Column A

_____ **1.** invented the steel-tipped plow

_____ **2.** clipper ship

_____ **3.** changed river travel

_____ **4.** steam-powered locomotive

_____ **5.** invented the sewing machine

Column B

A. Robert Fulton

B. the *Rocket*

C. John Deere

D. Elias Howe

E. the *Flying Cloud*

Short Answer   DIRECTIONS: Answer each question below in the space provided. *(10 points each)*

6. Innovations in what three areas changed the lives of Americans in the 1800s?

_____

7. What did manufacturers build so that products could be made more quickly?

_____

8. What opened new shipping routes by connecting many lakes and rivers?

_____

9. What invention made growing wheat more profitable?

_____

10. Who developed a code made of dots and dashes to transmit telegraphs?

_____

Name_____ Date_____ Class_____

Score: _____

Section Quiz 13-2

The North's People

Matching   DIRECTIONS: Match each item in Column A with an item in Column B. Write the correct letter in each blank. *(10 points each)*

Column A

_____ 1. extreme shortage of food

_____ 2. unfair opinion

_____ 3. unfair treatment of a group

_____ 4. founded Lowell Female Labor Reform Organization

_____ 5. wanted to decrease immigration

Column B

A. prejudice

B Know-Nothing Party

C. Sarah G. Bagley

D. famine

E. discrimination

Short Answer   DIRECTIONS: Answer each question below in the space provided. *(10 points each)*

6. What did long workdays and dangerous conditions within factories often lead to?

_____

_____

7. What is a trade union?

_____

_____

8. Why did so many Irish immigrants come to the United States between the 1840s and the 1860s?

_____

_____

9. What state court ruled that it was legal for workers to strike?

_____

10. What religious group were the nativists opposed to?

_____

Score: _____

Section Quiz 13-3
Southern Cotton Kingdom

Matching DIRECTIONS: Match each item in Column A with an item in Column B. Write the correct letter in each blank. *(10 points each)*

Column A

_____ 1. demanded by European mills

_____ 2. William Gregg

_____ 3. Eli Whitney

_____ 4. profitable colonial crop

_____ 5. money to invest

Column B

A. wanted to develop industry in the South

B. tobacco

C. capital

D. created the cotton gin

E. cotton

Short Answer DIRECTIONS: Answer each question below in the space provided. *(10 points each)*

6. In 1790 where did most Southerners live?

_____

_____

7. What was the cotton gin?

_____

_____

8. Why did the value of enslaved people increase in the 1860s?

_____

_____

9. How did the cotton gin increase production?

_____

_____

10. Why did some Southerners want to develop industry in the region?

_____

_____

Score: _____

Section Quiz 13-4

The South's People

Matching   DIRECTIONS: Match each item in Column A with an item in Column B. Write the correct letter in each blank. *(10 points each)*

Column A

Column B

_____ 1. farmers without enslaved people

A. tenant farmers

_____ 2. farmed landlords' estates

B. credit

_____ 3. lived in crude cabins

C. yeomen

_____ 4. to purchase goods with loaned money

D. overseer

_____ 5. plantation manager

E. rural poor

Short Answer   DIRECTIONS: Answer each question below in the space provided. *(10 points each)*

6. Most slaveholders held how many enslaved workers?

_____

_____

7. What did Congress outlaw in 1808?

_____

_____

8. Housing and feeding enslaved workers were considered what kind of costs?

_____

_____

9. What laws made it a crime to teach enslaved people to read and write?

_____

_____

10. What were some reasons for the South's low literacy rate?

_____

_____

Score: _____

Chapter 13 Test, Form A

North and South

Matching   DIRECTIONS: Match each item in Column A with an item in Column B. Write the correct letter in each blank. *(5 points each)*

Column A

_____ **1.** increased cotton processing

_____ **2.** plantation manager

_____ **3.** a form of loan

_____ **4.** refusal to work

_____ **5.** extreme shortage of food

Column B

A. credit

B. cotton gin

C. overseer

D. famine

E. strike

Multiple Choice   DIRECTIONS: In the blank, write the letter of the choice that best completes the statement or answers the question. *(8 points each)*

_____ **6.** Who constructed the first mechanical reaper?

    A. Cyrus McCormick   **C.** Samuel Morse

    B. Robert Fulton   **D.** John Deere

_____ **7.** Most enslaved people on plantations worked as

    A. domestics.   **C.** field hands.

    B. carpenters.   **D.** blacksmiths.

_____ **8.** Many immigrants lived in

    A. farm communities.   **C.** factory housing.

    B. slums.   **D.** rural areas.

_____ **9.** To put pressure on employers, workers staged

    A. famines.   **C.** trade unions.

    B. deteriorating conditions.   **D.** strikes.

_____ **10.** The main crop of the Deep South was

    A. sugarcane.   **C.** cotton.

    B. tobacco.   **D.** rice.

Test, Form A (continued)

DBQ **Document-Based Questions**   **DIRECTIONS:** Answer the questions in the space provided. *(10 points each)*

Transportation in the 1800s		
Year	**Type of Transportation**	**Description**
1807	steamboat	boat powered by steam that traveled along inland waterways
1825	omnibus	horse-drawn wagon that traveled city streets
1832	horsecar	horse-drawn wagon on rails that traveled city streets
1832	steam railroad	railroad systems that traveled locally for commuter traffic
1840	clipper ship	streamlined, fast-sailing ship for ocean travel
1867	cable car	railed streetcar attached to an overhead cable that moved under steam-powered engines

11. What is a horse-drawn wagon on rails called?

_____

_____

12. What is a streetcar that runs along a cable called?

_____

_____

Essay   **DIRECTIONS:** Answer the following question on a separate sheet of paper. *(15 points)*

13. In the South, what was the relationship between increased cotton production and the increased number of enslaved African Americans?

Score: _____

Chapter 13 Test, Form B

North and South

Matching **DIRECTIONS:** Match each item in Column A with an item in Column B. Write the correct letter in each blank. *(5 points each)*

Column A

Column B

_____ 1. built the first U.S. steam locomotive

A. Peter Cooper

_____ 2. transmitted the first telegraph message

B. fixed costs

_____ 3. enslaved African American who rebelled

C. nativists

_____ 4. regular expenses

D. Samuel Morse

_____ 5. formed American Party

E. Nat Turner

Multiple Choice **DIRECTIONS:** In the blank, write the letter of the choice that best completes the statement or answers the question. *(8 points each)*

_____ 6. Workers who had the same skills formed

    A. strikes.

    C. trade unions.

    B. famines.

    D. prejudices.

_____ 7. Famine caused people to immigrate to the United States from which country?

    A. Britain

    C. Spain

    B. Ireland

    D. Germany

_____ 8. Arriving between 1820 and 1860, the second-largest group of immigrants was from

    A. Britain.

    C. Spain.

    B. Ireland.

    D. Germany.

_____ 9. Which large group of Southerners owned small farms of about 50 to 200 acres?

    A. yeomen

    C. rural poor

    B. plantation owners

    D. tenant farmers

_____ 10. Who led a group of enslaved African Americans in rebellion against their slaveholders in 1831?

    A. Frederick Douglass

    C. Harriet Tubman

    B. Nat Turner

    D. Daniel Christian

Test, Form B (continued)

DBQ **Document-Based Questions** **DIRECTIONS:** Answer the questions in the space provided. *(10 points each)*

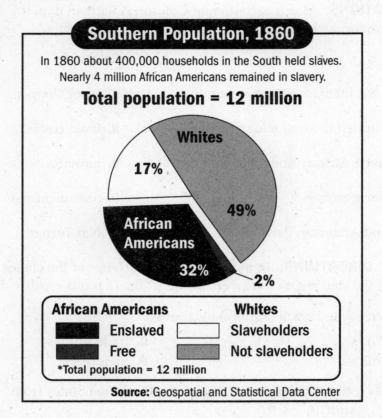

Southern Population, 1860

In 1860 about 400,000 households in the South held slaves. Nearly 4 million African Americans remained in slavery.

Total population = 12 million

Whites

17%

49%

African Americans

32%

2%

African Americans		Whites	
■ Enslaved	□ Slaveholders		
■ Free	▨ Not slaveholders		

*Total population = 12 million

Source: Geospatial and Statistical Data Center

_____ **11.** About what percentage of the Southern population in 1860 was enslaved African Americans?

　　A. about one-third　　　　　**C.** about one-half

　　B. about one-quarter　　　　**D.** about two-thirds

_____ **12.** About what percentage of the Southern population in 1860 was nonslaveholding whites?

　　A. about one-third　　　　　**C.** about one-half

　　B. about one-quarter　　　　**D.** about two-thirds

Essay **DIRECTIONS:** Answer the following question on a separate sheet of paper. *(15 points)*

13. What were the barriers to industry in the South?

Score: _____

Chapter 13 Test, Form C
North and South

Matching **DIRECTIONS:** Match each item in Column A with an item in Column B. Write the correct letter in each blank. *(5 points each)*

Column A

Column B

_____ 1. the North's main source of income

A. industry

_____ 2. the South's main source of income

B. Upper South

_____ 3. members of the Know-Nothing Party

C. Deep South

_____ 4. grew sugarcane

D. agriculture

_____ 5. produced tobacco

E. nativists

Multiple Choice **DIRECTIONS:** In the blank, write the letter of the choice that best completes the statement or answers the question. *(8 points each)*

_____ 6. By 1860, the Midwest and the East were united by a network of

    A. roads.

    C. canals.

    B. railroad tracks.

    D. steam-powered ships.

_____ 7. The demand for cotton from the South came from mills in

    A. Mexico.

    C. Europe.

    B. the North.

    D. Asia.

_____ 8. A shortage of what would have devastating consequences for the South during the Civil War?

    A. canals

    C. rivers

    B. railroads

    D. roads

_____ 9. Which of the following transformed trade in the nation's interior?

    A. clipper ships

    C. railways

    B. telegraphs

    D. sewing machines

_____ 10. What did the thriving economy of the South depend on?

    A. tobacco

    C. slavery

    B. rice

    D. railroads

DBQ **Document-Based Questions** **DIRECTIONS:** Answer the questions
in the space provided. *(10 points each)*

Transportation in the 1800s		
Year	**Type of Transportation**	**Description**
1807	steamboat	boat powered by steam that traveled along inland waterways
1825	omnibus	horse-drawn wagon that traveled city streets
1832	horsecar	horse-drawn wagon on rails that traveled city streets
1832	steam railroad	railroad systems that traveled locally for commuter traffic
1840	clipper ship	streamlined, fast-sailing ship for ocean travel
1867	cable car	railed streetcar attached to an overhead cable that moved under steam-powered engines

11. What were the differences between clipper ships and steamboats?

_____

_____

12. What were the differences between omnibuses and horsecars?

_____

_____

Essay **DIRECTIONS:** Answer the following question on a separate sheet
of paper. *(15 points)*

13. What are two examples of how racial prejudice and discrimination
remained in the North, even though slavery had mostly disappeared in
Northern states by 1820?

Section Quiz 14-1
Social Reform

Matching DIRECTIONS: Match each item in Column A with an item in Column B. Write the correct letter in each blank. *(10 points each)*

Column A

_____ **1.** perfect society

_____ **2.** wave of religious fervor

_____ **3.** religious camp meetings

_____ **4.** leader of educational reform

_____ **5.** poet

Column B

A. Second Great Awakening

B. Horace Mann

C. utopia

D. Walt Whitman

E. revivals

Short Answer DIRECTIONS: Answer each question below in the space provided. *(10 points each)*

6. What is the name of the first college in the United States to admit women and African Americans?

_____

7. What is civil disobedience?

_____

_____

8. What group of people with special needs did Samuel Howe help?

_____

_____

9. What did the transcendentalists write about?

_____

_____

10. What is temperance?

_____

_____

Score: _____

Section Quiz 14-2
The Abolitionists

Matching   DIRECTIONS: Match each item in Column A with an item in
Column B. Write the correct letter in each blank. *(10 points each)*

Column A

_____ **1.** worked to end slavery

_____ **2.** American Colonization Society colony

_____ **3.** founded *The Liberator*

_____ **4.** a Southerner against slavery

_____ **5.** "Belle"

Column B

A. William Lloyd Garrison

B. Sojourner Truth

C. Angelina Grimké

D. abolitionists

E. Liberia

Short Answer   DIRECTIONS: Answer each question below in the space
provided. *(10 points each)*

6. What were two weaknesses of the American Colonization Society?

_____

_____

7. Name the sisters who were among the first women to speak out publicly
against slavery.

_____

_____

8. What name was given to the network of escape routes used by slaves to
get from the South to freedom in the North?

_____

9. Who was killed by angry whites at his newspaper office?

_____

10. Define *abolitionists.*

_____

_____

Score: _____

Section Quiz 14-3

The Women's Movement

Matching DIRECTIONS: Match each item in Column A with an item in Column B. Write the correct letter in each blank. *(10 points each)*

Column A

_____ **1.** first Americans to work for women's rights

_____ **2.** organized Philadelphia Female Anti-Slavery Society

_____ **3.** Seneca Falls, New York

_____ **4.** right to vote

_____ **5.** organized Daughters of Temperance

Column B

A. Lucretia Mott

B. site of first women's rights convention

C. suffrage

D. Susan B. Anthony

E. women abolitionists

Short Answer DIRECTIONS: Answer each question below in the space provided. *(10 points each)*

6. In what year did women gain the right to vote throughout the entire United States?

_____

7. Name the document that was issued by the Seneca Falls Convention.

_____

_____

8. Name the women's rights leader who called for coeducation.

_____

9. What school did Mary Lyon establish in 1837?

_____

10. Which state was the first to grant woman suffrage in 1890?

_____

_____

Score: _____

Chapter 14 Test, Form A
The Age of Reform

Matching   DIRECTIONS: Match each item in Column A with an item in Column B. Write the correct letter in each blank. *(5 points each)*

Column A

Column B

_____ **1.** teaching males and females together

A. temperance

_____ **2.** the right to vote

B. suffrage

_____ **3.** reformer working to end slavery

C. revival

_____ **4.** frontier camp meeting

D. abolitionist

_____ **5.** drinking little or no alcohol

E. coeducation

Multiple Choice   DIRECTIONS: In the blank, write the letter of the choice that best completes the statement or answers the question. *(8 points each)*

_____ **6.** A community based on a vision of the perfect society is called a

    A. revival.
    B. frontier camp.
    C. utopia.
    D. college.

_____ **7.** What was the name of the former enslaved African American who attracted huge crowds to hear her eloquent speeches?

    A. Sojourner Truth
    B. Dorothea Dix
    C. Harriet Tubman
    D. Sarah Grimké

_____ **8.** In the 1800s, there was a wave of religious fervor known as the

    A. Religious Right.
    B. Second Great Awakening.
    C. Religious Awakening.
    D. Revival Times.

_____ **9.** The network of escape routes out of the South for enslaved people was the

    A. Escape Network.
    B. Slave Network.
    C. Underground Railroad.
    D. Southern Escape Route.

_____ **10.** Who was the most famous person who helped runaway slaves reach freedom?

    A. Sojourner Truth
    B. Angelina Grimké
    C. Harriet Tubman
    D. Sarah Grimké

Test, Form A (continued)

DBQ **Document-Based Questions** **DIRECTIONS:** Answer the questions in the space provided. *(10 points each)*

Author	James Fenimore Cooper	Washington Irving	Nathaniel Hawthorne	Herman Melville	Edgar Allan Poe	Harriet Beecher Stowe
Birth	1789	1783	1804	1819	1809	1811
Death	1851	1859	1864	1891	1849	1896
Major Work	*The Last of the Mohicans*	*The Legend of Sleepy Hollow*	*The Scarlet Letter*	*Moby Dick*	*The Tell-Tale Heart*	*Uncle Tom's Cabin*
Year Published	1826	1819	1850	1851	1843	1852

11. How many of these authors lived in two different centuries?

_____

_____

12. Which authors lived only in the 1800s?

_____

_____

Essay **DIRECTIONS:** Answer the following question on a separate sheet of paper. *(15 points)*

13. During the 1800s, what gains did women make concerning marriage and property laws?

Score: _____

Chapter 14 Test, Form B

The Age of Reform

Matching DIRECTIONS: Match each item in Column A with an item in Column B. Write the correct letter in each blank. *(5 points each)*

Column A

_____ **1.** wrote *Uncle Tom's Cabin*

_____ **2.** reformed care for mentally ill

_____ **3.** runaway slave escape route

_____ **4.** demanded woman suffrage

_____ **5.** *North Star* editor

Column B

A. Frederick Douglass

B. Harriet Beecher Stowe

C. Underground Railroad

D. Elizabeth Cady Stanton

E. Dorothea Dix

Multiple Choice DIRECTIONS: In the blank, write the letter of the choice that best completes the statement or answers the question. *(8 points each)*

_____ **6.** Who was a leader of educational reform?

    A. Lyman Beecher

    B. Horace Mann

    C. Charles Finney

    D. Dorothea Dix

_____ **7.** The first white abolitionist to call for the "immediate and complete emancipation" of enslaved people was

    A. Benjamin Lundy.

    B. William Lloyd Garrison.

    C. David Walker.

    D. Frederick Douglass.

_____ **8.** The first women's rights convention was held in

    A. Georgia.

    B. New York.

    C. Virginia.

    D. Ohio.

_____ **9.** Who purchased his freedom from the slaveholder from whom he fled?

    A. Frederick Douglass

    B. Horace Mann

    C. Charles T. Weber

    D. Theodore Weld

_____ **10.** Who graduated first in the class and gained fame as a doctor after being repeatedly turned down for admission to medical school?

    A. Theodore Weld

    B. Frederick Douglass

    C. Susan B. Anthony

    D. Elizabeth Blackwell

Test, Form B (continued)

DBQ **Document-Based Questions** **DIRECTIONS:** Answer the questions in the space provided. *(10 points each)*

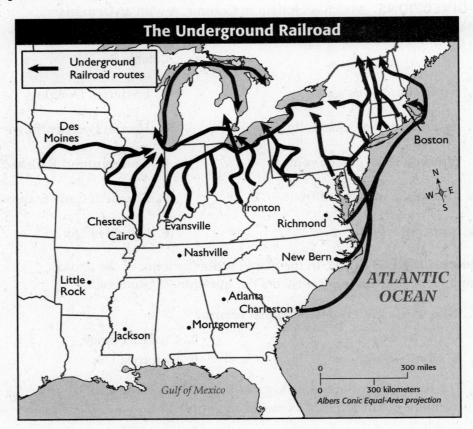

The Underground Railroad

Underground Railroad routes

Des Moines
Boston
Chester
Cairo
Evansville
Ironton
Richmond
Nashville
New Bern
Little Rock
ATLANTIC OCEAN
Atlanta
Charleston
Jackson
Montgomery

0   300 miles
0   300 kilometers
Albers Conic Equal-Area projection

Gulf of Mexico

_____ **11.** About how many miles did an enslaved person travel from Charleston, South Carolina, to Boston, Massachusetts?

  A. about 300 miles   **C.** about 800 miles

  B. about 600 miles   **D.** about 1,100 miles

_____ **12.** In general, in which direction did Underground Railroad routes travel?

  A. north   **C.** east

  B. south   **D.** west

Essay **DIRECTIONS:** Answer the following question on a separate sheet of paper. *(15 points)*

13. How were writers influential in many of the reform movements of the 1800s?

Score: _____

Chapter 14 Test, Form C
The Age of Reform

Matching   DIRECTIONS: Match each item in Column A with an item in Column B. Write the correct letter in each blank. *(5 points each)*

Column A

_____ **1.** perfect society

_____ **2.** founder of Troy Female Seminary

_____ **3.** founder of Mount Holyoke

_____ **4.** Liberia

_____ **5.** practiced civil disobedience

Column B

A. utopia

B. Henry David Thoreau

C. Mary Lyon

D. Emma Willard

E. "place of freedom"

Multiple Choice   DIRECTIONS: In the blank, write the letter of the choice that best completes the statement or answers the question. *(8 points each)*

_____ **6.** Writers Margaret Fuller, Ralph Waldo Emerson, and Henry David Thoreau were

    A. enslaved people.

    B. utopians.

    C. revivalists.

    D. transcendentalists.

_____ **7.** Women fighting to end slavery recognized their own oppression and formed the

    A. temperance movement.

    B. education movement.

    C. suffrage movement.

    D. women's rights movement.

_____ **8.** Which movement called for drinking little or no alcohol?

    A. transcendentalist

    B. utopia communities

    C. temperance

    D. reformers

_____ **9.** Who wrote the narrative poem *Song of Hiawatha*?

    A. Ralph Waldo Emerson

    B. Emily Dickinson

    C. Henry Wadsworth Longfellow

    D. Margaret Fuller

_____ **10.** The most controversial issue at the Seneca Falls convention concerned

    A. education.

    B. suffrage.

    C. jobs.

    D. slavery.

Test, Form C (continued)

DBQ **Document-Based Questions** **DIRECTIONS:** Answer the questions in the space provided. *(10 points each)*

> "Section 1. *Be it enacted by the Senate and House of Representatives, in General Court assembled, and by the authority of the same,* that each town or district within this Commonwealth containing 50 families or householders shall be provided with a teacher or teachers, of good morals, to instruct children in orthography, reading, writing, English grammar, geography, arithmetic, and good behavior, for such term of time as shall be equivalent to six months for one school in each year. . . ."
>
> — state legislature of Massachusetts, 1827

_____ **11.** This excerpt is an early example of a law that

    A. required parents to pay for schooling.

    B. encouraged teacher training.

    C. provided public schools.

    D. set up school taxes.

12. Given what you know about education in this time period, who might not have benefited from this law and why?

_____

_____

Essay **DIRECTIONS:** Answer the following question on a separate sheet of paper. *(15 points)*

13. What was the American Colonization Society, and why did it not work?

Name_____ Date_____ Class_____

Section Quiz 15-1

Slavery and the West

Matching DIRECTIONS: Match each item in Column A with an item in Column B. Write the correct letter in each blank. *(10 points each)*

Column A

_____ **1.** slave state

_____ **2.** free state

_____ **3.** Free-Soil Party candidate

_____ **4.** runaway slaves

_____ **5.** to leave the Union

Column B

A. Maine

B. Missouri

C. fugitives

D. secede

E. Martin Van Buren

Short Answer DIRECTIONS: Answer each question below in the space provided. *(10 points each)*

6. In 1819 what was the balance in Congress between slave states and free states?

_____

_____

7. With the Missouri Compromise, what state was admitted to the Union as a free state to preserve the balance of power?

_____

8. What was the Wilmot Proviso?

_____

_____

9. What was the slogan of the Free-Soil Party?

_____

10. What compromise was made regarding slavery in Washington, D.C.?

_____

_____

Score: _____

Section Quiz 15-2

A Nation Dividing

Matching   DIRECTIONS: Match each item in Column A with an item in
Column B. Write the correct letter in each blank. *(10 points each)*

Column A

_____ **1.** bought freedom of enslaved people

_____ **2.** boundary of slavery

_____ **3.** allowing the people to decide

_____ **4.** fighting between pro-slavery
and antislavery forces

_____ **5.** violent abolitionist

Column B

A. 36°30′ N latitude

B. "Bleeding Kansas"

C. John Brown

D. popular sovereignty

E. antislavery groups

Short Answer   DIRECTIONS: Answer each question below in the space
provided. *(10 points each)*

6. What unintended effect did the Fugitive Slave Act have on Northerners?

_____

_____

7. Name the writer who encouraged people to break unjust laws in his
essay "Civil Disobedience."

_____

8. What was the name of the armed pro-slavery groups of Missourians who
went to Kansas to vote?

_____

9. What was the response of antislavery forces in Kansas after the new
Kansas legislature passed pro-slavery laws?

_____

_____

10. What happened in the town of Lawrence, Kansas, in May 1856?

_____

_____

Score: _____

Section Quiz 15-3
Challenges to Slavery

Matching   DIRECTIONS: Match each item in Column A with an item in Column B. Write the correct letter in each blank. *(10 points each)*

Column A

_____ **1.** sued for freedom

_____ **2.** a person who dies for a cause

_____ **3.** arsenal

_____ **4.** 1856 Know-Nothing candidate

_____ **5.** "the Little Giant"

Column B

A. martyr

B. Millard Fillmore

C. Stephen A. Douglas

D. Dred Scott

E. storage site for weapons

Short Answer   DIRECTIONS: Answer each question below in the space provided. *(10 points each)*

6. Which groups joined together in 1854 to form the Republican Party?

_____

_____

7. Who were the candidates for president in the election of 1856?

_____

_____

8. For what reason did Dred Scott claim that he should be free?

_____

_____

9. Who was chief justice of the United States for the *Dred Scott* ruling?

_____

_____

10. What did John Brown hope to accomplish with his raid on the arsenal at Harpers Ferry, Virginia?

_____

_____

Section Quiz 15-4

Secession and War

Matching   DIRECTIONS: Match each item in Column A with an item in Column B. Write the correct letter in each blank. *(10 points each)*

Column A

_____ 1. Republican candidate

_____ 2. one of the first states to secede

_____ 3. candidate of Southern Democrats

_____ 4. April 14, 1861

_____ 5. proposed last-minute compromise

Column B

A. John Breckinridge

B. Abraham Lincoln

C. John Crittenden

D. Virginia

E. Fort Sumter surrender

Short Answer   DIRECTIONS: Answer each question below in the space provided. *(10 points each)*

6. How many candidates ran for president in the election of 1860?

_____

7. How did Lincoln win the election when his name was not even on the ballot in some Southern states?

_____

_____

8. What did Southerners fear would result from the Republican victory?

_____

_____

9. What was the name of the new nation formed by the states that seceded from the Union?

_____

10. What event officially started the Civil War?

_____

Score: _____

Chapter 15 Test, Form A
Toward Civil War

Matching DIRECTIONS: Match each item in Column A with an item in Column B. Write the correct letter in each blank. *(5 points each)*

Column A

Column B

_____ **1.** president of the Confederacy

A. popular sovereignty

_____ **2.** letting the people decide

B. John C. Frémont

_____ **3.** Republican candidate in 1856

C. Confederacy

_____ **4.** formed on February 4, 1861

D. Fort Sumter

_____ **5.** first attack of the Civil War

E. Jefferson Davis

Multiple Choice DIRECTIONS: In the blank, write the letter of the choice that best completes the statement or answers the question. *(8 points each)*

_____ **6.** Henry Clay's compromise became known as
  A. the Maine Compromise.   **C.** Clay's Compromise.
  B. the Missouri Compromise.   **D.** Henry's Compromise.

_____ **7.** Southerners justified secession with the theory of
  A. constitutional rights.   **C.** the Union's errors.
  B. federal rights.   **D.** states' rights.

_____ **8.** The main issue in the election of 1844 was the annexation of
  A. Texas.   **C.** Missouri.
  B. Kansas.   **D.** California.

_____ **9.** According to the _____, a person could be fined or imprisoned for aiding fugitives.
  A. Southern Slave Act   **C.** Fugitive Slave Act
  B. Owners-Right Act   **D.** Runaway Slave Act

_____ **10.** Douglas's stand that people could exclude slavery by refusing to pass laws protecting slaveholders' rights came to be known as
  A. Douglas's Debate.   **C.** the Freeport Doctrine.
  B. the Slaveholder's Rights.   **D.** Douglas's Doctrine.

Test, Form A (continued)

DBQ **Document-Based Questions**   **DIRECTIONS:** Answer the questions
in the space provided. *(10 points each)*

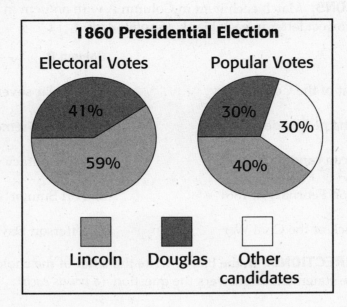

1860 Presidential Election

Electoral Votes

Popular Votes

Lincoln   Douglas   Other candidates

11. According to the graphs, who won the most electoral votes?

_____

_____

12. Who won 41 percent of the electoral vote?

_____

_____

Essay   **DIRECTIONS:** Answer the following question on a separate sheet
of paper. *(15 points)*

13. What did the Missouri Compromise propose, and what was the result?

Score: _____

Chapter 15 Test, Form B

Toward Civil War

Matching **DIRECTIONS:** Match each item in Column A with an item in Column B. Write the correct letter in each blank. *(5 points each)*

Column A

_____ **1.** proposed Missouri Compromise

_____ **2.** violent abolitionist

_____ **3.** opponent of Abraham Lincoln

_____ **4.** won the 1848 presidential election

_____ **5.** ruled on *Dred Scott* decision

Column B

A. Stephen A. Douglas

B. Henry Clay

C. John Brown

D. Roger B. Taney

E. Zachary Taylor

Multiple Choice **DIRECTIONS:** In the blank, write the letter of the choice that best completes the statement or answers the question. *(8 points each)*

_____ **6.** Which party endorsed the Wilmot Proviso?

    A. Whig   **C.** Democratic
    B. Free-Soil   **D.** Republican

_____ **7.** What did Franklin Pierce become in 1853?

    A. senator   **C.** a fugitive
    B. editor of *The Liberator*   **D.** president

_____ **8.** In the congressional election of 1858, the Senate race in which state was the center of national attention?

    A. Illinois   **C.** Indiana
    B. Michigan   **D.** Ohio

_____ **9.** Which Supreme Court decision divided the nation even more?

    A. Fugitive Slave case   **C.** Clay's ruling
    B. *Dred Scott* case   **D.** *John Brown* case

_____ **10.** Who was the senator from Kentucky who tried to save the Union by proposing a last-minute compromise?

    A. John Calhoun   **C.** John Crittenden
    B. John Bell   **D.** Henry Clay

Test, Form B (continued)

DBQ Document-Based Questions **DIRECTIONS:** Answer the questions in the space provided. *(10 points each)*

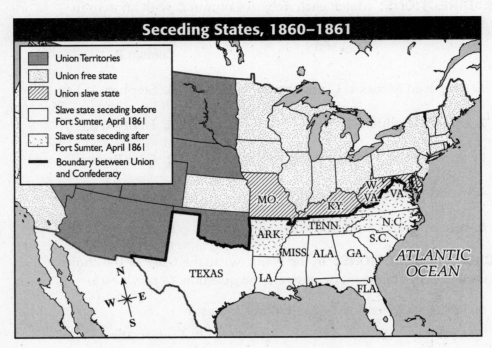

Seceding States, 1860–1861

Legend:
- Union Territories
- Union free state
- Union slave state
- Slave state seceding before Fort Sumter, April 1861
- Slave state seceding after Fort Sumter, April 1861
- Boundary between Union and Confederacy

_____ 11. According to the map, in 1860 Kentucky and West Virginia were both

　　A. Union free states.　　　　　　C. Union territories.

　　B. slave states.　　　　　　　　D. Union slave states.

_____ 12. How many states seceded after April 1861?

　　A. 11　　　　　　　　　　　C. 6

　　B. 10　　　　　　　　　　　D. 4

Essay **DIRECTIONS:** Answer the following question on a separate sheet of paper. *(15 points)*

13. How did sectionalism lead to the Civil War?

Score: _____

Chapter 15 Test, Form C
Toward Civil War

Matching   DIRECTIONS: Match each item in Column A with an item in Column B. Write the correct letter in each blank. *(5 points each)*

Column A

_____ **1.** Henry Clay's plan

_____ **2.** wrote essay "Civil Disobedience"

_____ **3.** Stephen Douglas's response to slavery

_____ **4.** repealed the Missouri Compromise

_____ **5.** proposed amendments to protect slavery

Column B

A. Henry David Thoreau

B. Kansas-Nebraska Act

C. John Crittenden

D. Freeport Doctrine

E. Missouri Compromise

Multiple Choice   DIRECTIONS: In the blank, write the letter of the choice that best completes the statement or answers the question. *(8 points each)*

_____ **6.** The admission of Missouri as a slave state was controversial in the Senate because

    A. the Senate was pro-slavery.

    B. it would create sectionalism.

    C. it would upset the balance.

    D. the Senate was antislavery.

_____ **7.** Enforcement of the Fugitive Act led to

    A. compromise.

    B. more anger in the North.

    C. recognition of Southerners' rights.

    D. an end to the struggle.

_____ **8.** The main topic of the Lincoln–Douglas debates was

    A. Western territories.

    B. war with Mexico.

    C. slavery.

    D. the economy.

_____ **9.** Who won the presidential election of 1860?

    A. John C. Calhoun

    B. John Bell

    C. Abraham Lincoln

    D. John Breckinridge

_____ **10.** Which plan specified that slavery should be prohibited in any lands that might be acquired from Mexico?

    A. Missouri Compromise

    B. Clay's Plan

    C. Mexican Plan

    D. Wilmot Proviso

Test, Form C (continued)

DBQ **Document-Based Questions** **DIRECTIONS:** Answer the questions in the space provided. *(10 points each)*

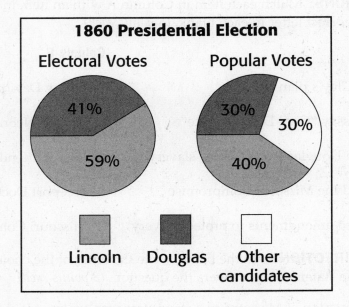

1860 Presidential Election

Electoral Votes

- 41%
- 59%

Popular Votes

- 30%
- 30%
- 40%

Lincoln Douglas Other candidates

11. Why did Lincoln, who got less than 50 percent of the popular vote, win the election?

_____

_____

12. The Democratic Party was split into two factions. What issue divided the party and allowed Lincoln to win the majority?

_____

_____

Essay **DIRECTIONS:** Answer the following question on a separate sheet of paper. *(15 points)*

13. How did the idea of popular sovereignty in the Kansas and Nebraska territories contradict the Missouri Compromise of 1820?

Name_____ Date_____ Class_____

Section Quiz 16-1
The Two Sides

Matching DIRECTIONS: Match each item in Column A with an item in Column B. Write the correct letter in each blank. *(10 points each)*

Column A

_____ **1.** Confederate capital

_____ **2.** Union's first strategy

_____ **3.** sell to other countries

_____ **4.** Confederate soldiers

_____ **5.** Union soldiers

Column B

A. export

B. Yankees

C. Rebels

D. Richmond, Virginia

E. blockade Southern ports

Short Answer DIRECTIONS: Answer each question below in the space provided. *(10 points each)*

6. Why was the border state of Maryland vital to the Union?

_____

_____

7. Which plan of the South's was not a defensive strategy?

_____

_____

8. The North's war plan came from which hero of the war with Mexico?

_____

9. Name the North's plan to gain control of the Mississippi River.

_____

10. About 1 of every 11 Union soldiers ran away because of fear, hunger, or sickness. How many Confederate soldiers ran away?

_____

_____

Score:_____

Section Quiz 16-2

Early Stages of the War

Matching   DIRECTIONS: Match each item in Column A with an item in Column B. Write the correct letter in each blank. *(10 points each)*

Column A

_____ **1.** Confederate general

_____ **2.** *Merrimack*

_____ **3.** people killed or wounded

_____ **4.** Union general at Shiloh

_____ **5.** abolitionist orator

Column B

A. casualties

B. "Stonewall" Jackson

C. ironclad ship

D. Frederick Douglass

E. Ulysses S. Grant

Short Answer   DIRECTIONS: Answer each question below in the space provided. *(10 points each)*

6. Who was the Union general who captured Fort Henry?

_____

7. Why did the Union want to control the Mississippi River and its tributaries?

_____

_____

8. Which side won the Battle of Shiloh?

_____

9. What constitutional right did Lincoln have to free enslaved African Americans in the South?

_____

_____

10. What was the Emancipation Proclamation?

_____

_____

Section Quiz 16-3

Life During the War

Matching   DIRECTIONS: Match each item in Column A with an item in Column B. Write the correct letter in each blank. *(10 points each)*

Column A

_____ **1.** general increase in prices

_____ **2.** Southern spy

_____ **3.** first woman army surgeon

_____ **4.** Copperheads

_____ **5.** payments to encourage enlistment

Column B

A. Mary Edwards Walker

B. Peace Democrats

C. Rose O'Neal Greenhow

D. bounties

E. inflation

Short Answer   DIRECTIONS: Answer each question below in the space provided. *(10 points each)*

6. What types of shortages did the South experience during the Civil War?

_____

_____

7. What were the two roles of women who were actively involved in the war?

_____

8. Why was disease so common for soldiers on both sides of the fight?

_____

_____

9. Who were the Copperheads, and what position did they take on the war?

_____

_____

10. Define *integrate*.

_____

_____

Name_____ Date_____ Class_____

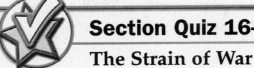

Section Quiz 16-4

The Strain of War

Matching DIRECTIONS: Match each item in Column A with an item in Column B. Write the correct letter in each blank. *(10 points each)*

Column A

_____ **1.** Gettysburg Address

_____ **2.** site of Pickett's Charge

_____ **3.** in a protected position

_____ **4.** took place on July 4th, 1863

_____ **5.** African American regiment

Column B

A. entrenched

B. 272 words

C. surrender of Vicksburg

D. 54th Massachusetts

E. Battle of Gettysburg

Short Answer DIRECTIONS: Answer each question below in the space provided. *(10 points each)*

6. How did General Stonewall Jackson die?

_____

_____

7. What was the "last straw" with President Lincoln regarding General McClellan?

_____

_____

8. What was the Amnesty Act?

_____

_____

9. After the Battle of Gettysburg, what did Britain withhold from the South?

_____

_____

10. How long did the siege of Vicksburg last?

_____

Score: _____

Section Quiz 16-5

The War's Final Stages

Matching   DIRECTIONS: Match each item in Column A with an item in Column B. Write the correct letter in each blank. *(10 points each)*

Column A

_____ **1.** freed enslaved Americans

_____ **2.** action plan

_____ **3.** trail of destruction

_____ **4.** commander of the Union armies

_____ **5.** Union navy hero

Column B

A. March to the Sea

B. Ulysses S. Grant

C. strategy

D. David Farragut

E. Thirteenth Amendment

Short Answer   DIRECTIONS: Answer each question below in the space provided. *(10 points each)*

6. Whose strategy was the total war in Atlanta?

_____

7. Why was Petersburg important to the Confederacy and a prime target for the Union?

_____

_____

8. What helped Lincoln win the 1864 election?

_____

_____

9. What happened in Richmond after Lee's retreat at Petersburg?

_____

10. What was Reconstruction?

_____

_____

Score: _____

Chapter 16 Test, Form A

The Civil War

Matching   DIRECTIONS: Match each item in Column A with an item in Column B. Write the correct letter in each blank. *(5 points each)*

Column A

_____ **1.** Union capital

_____ **2.** South's ironclad ship

_____ **3.** to close ports

_____ **4.** era after the war

_____ **5.** Northern money

Column B

A. *Merrimack*

B. greenbacks

C. blockade

D. Washington, D.C.

E. Reconstruction

Multiple Choice   DIRECTIONS: In the blank, write the letter of the choice that best completes the statement or answers the question. *(8 points each)*

_____ **6.** The bloodiest day of the entire Civil War was the Battle of

  A. Shiloh.

  B. Antietam.

  C. Richmond.

  D. New Orleans.

_____ **7.** In the Civil War, for the first time, thousands of women served as

  A. soldiers.

  B. spies.

  C. generals.

  D. nurses.

_____ **8.** "Peace Democrats" became known as

  A. War Hawks.

  B. Rebels.

  C. Copperheads.

  D. Radicals.

_____ **9.** The plan to gain control of the Mississippi River and split the Confederacy in two was called

  A. the Anaconda Plan.

  B. the Squeeze Play.

  C. the Great Divide.

  D. the River Conquest.

_____ **10.** On January 1, 1863, President Abraham Lincoln signed the

  A. Free Slave Bill.

  B. Fourteenth Amendment.

  C. Emancipation Proclamation.

  D. Thirteenth Amendment.

Test, Form A (continued)

DBQ **Document-Based Questions** **DIRECTIONS:** Answer the questions in the space provided. *(10 points each)*

> "... That on the first day of January, in the year of our Lord one thousand eight hundred and sixty-three, all persons held as slaves within any state or designated part of a state, the people whereof shall then be in rebellion against the United States, shall be then, thenceforward, and forever, free; and the Executive Government of the United States, including the military and naval authority thereof, will recognize and maintain the freedom of such persons, and will do no act or acts to repress such persons, or any of them, in any efforts they may make for their actual freedom. ..."

_____ **11.** This announcement by the president of the United States is a quotation from

    A. the Constitution.
    B. the Emancipation Proclamation.
    C. the Gettysburg Address.
    D. the Thirteenth Amendment.

_____ **12.** According to this excerpt, who will help the former enslaved people gain their freedom?

    A. plantation owners
    B. the president
    C. the executive government
    D. No one will assist.

Essay **DIRECTIONS:** Answer the following question on a separate sheet of paper. *(15 points)*

13. How would the Emancipation Proclamation have changed the life of an enslaved African American in Maryland?

Score: _____

Chapter 16 Test, Form B

The Civil War

Matching **DIRECTIONS:** Match each item in Column A with an item in Column B. Write the correct letter in each blank. *(5 points each)*

Column A

Column B

_____ **1.** captured New Orleans

A. Richmond, Virginia

_____ **2.** 54th Massachusetts

B. African American regiment

_____ **3.** site of Robert E. Lee's surrender

C. Appomattox Court House

_____ **4.** Confederate capital

D. Jefferson Davis

_____ **5.** Confederate president

E. David Farragut

Multiple Choice **DIRECTIONS:** In the blank, write the letter of the choice that best completes the statement or answers the question. *(8 points each)*

_____ **6.** Because the war disrupted their supply of cotton, the South expected support from

    A. France and Spain.

    B. Spain and Mexico.

    C. France and Canada.

    D. Britain and France.

_____ **7.** What battle was named after a small church?

    A. Shiloh

    B. Gettysburg

    C. Vicksburg

    D. Atlanta

_____ **8.** What battle began July 1, 1863, when the Confederates entered a town for supplies and encountered Union troops?

    A. Shiloh

    B. Gettysburg

    C. Vicksburg

    D. Richmond

_____ **9.** Who expressed his opinion to Lincoln that by casting the war as a fight against slavery, European countries would be less likely to aid the South?

    A. Frederick Douglass

    B. David Farragut

    C. George B. McClellan

    D. Ulysses S. Grant

_____ **10.** Pickett's Charge took place during the Battle of

    A. Shiloh.

    B. Chancellorsville.

    C. Gettysburg.

    D. Fredericksburg.

Test, Form B (continued)

DBQ Document-Based Questions DIRECTIONS: Answer the questions in the space provided. *(10 points each)*

> "A cruel, crazy, mad, hopeless panic possessed them. . . . The heat was awful . . . the men were exhausted—their mouths gaped, their lips cracked and blackened with the powder of the cartridges they had bitten off in the battle, their eyes staring in frenzy."
>
> —*Representative Albert Riddle, observing the First Battle of Bull Run*

_____ **11.** This excerpt describes _____ at the First Battle of Bull Run.

   A. terrified observers

   B. courageous Confederate soldiers

   C. retreating Union soldiers

   D. civilians fleeing to Washington, D.C.

> ". . . It had suddenly appeared to him that perhaps in a battle he might run. He was forced to admit that as far as war was concerned he knew nothing of himself. . . .
>
> "A little panic-fear grew in his mind. As his imagination went forward to a fight, he saw hideous possibilities. . . ."
>
> —*Stephen Crane, The Red Badge of Courage*

12. What words in the excerpt tell you the character was afraid?

_____

_____

Essay DIRECTIONS: Answer the following question on a separate sheet of paper. *(15 points)*

13. List the border states, and explain why they were so important to the Union.

Score: _____

Chapter 16 Test, Form C
The Civil War

Matching **DIRECTIONS:** Match each item in Column A with an item in Column B. Write the correct letter in each blank. *(5 points each)*

Column A

_____ **1.** total war

_____ **2.** prisoner's right

_____ **3.** Peace Democrats

_____ **4.** Confederate commander

_____ **5.** casualty of Chancellorsville

Column B

A. habeas corpus

B. Sherman's strategy

C. General P.G.T. Beauregard

D. Copperheads

E. Stonewall Jackson

Multiple Choice **DIRECTIONS:** In the blank, write the letter of the choice that best completes the statement or answers the question. *(8 points each)*

_____ **6.** The North's war plan came from a hero of the war with Mexico named

    A. Winfield Scott.
    B. George McClellan.
    C. Abraham Lincoln.
    D. Robert E. Lee.

_____ **7.** The main goal of the North at the beginning of the war was to

    A. end slavery.
    B. be recognized as independent.
    C. punish the South.
    D. reunite the country.

_____ **8.** General P.G.T. Beauregard fought against General Irvin McDowell at

    A. Shiloh.
    B. Gettysburg.
    C. the First Battle of Bull Run.
    D. the Second Battle of Bull Run.

_____ **9.** The battle of the *Monitor* and the *Merrimack* was the first ever between

    A. cutters.
    B. ironclad ships.
    C. warships.
    D. clippers.

_____ **10.** Appomattox Court House is famous because it is the site of

    A. a bloody battle.
    B. Union headquarters.
    C. Confederate headquarters.
    D. Robert E. Lee's surrender.

Test, Form C (continued)

DBQ Document-Based Questions **DIRECTIONS:** Answer the questions in the space provided. *(10 points each)*

> "July 29, 1864—Sleepless nights. The report is that the Yankees have left Covington for Macon, . . . to release prisoners held there. They robbed every house on the road of its provisions [supplies], sometimes taking every piece of meat, blankets and wearing apparel, silver and arms of every description. They would take silk dresses and put them under their saddles, and many other things for which they had no use. Is this the way to make us love them and their Union? Let the poor people answer [those] whom they have deprived of every mouthful of meat and of their livestock to make any! Our mills, too, they have burned, destroying an immense amount of property."
>
> —from the diary of Dolly Sumner Lunt

_____ **11.** During General Sherman's March to the Sea, described in this excerpt, the object of this destruction was

   A. to destroy the Confederate army.

   B. to find supplies for the Union army.

   C. to encourage freeing the South's slaves.

   D. to break the South's will to fight.

12. What is Lunt's attitude toward the Yankees and why?

_____

_____

Essay DIRECTIONS: Answer the following question on a separate sheet of paper. *(15 points)*

13. What made President Abraham Lincoln decide to emancipate enslaved African Americans?

Score: _____

Section Quiz 17-1
Reconstruction Plans

Matching **DIRECTIONS:** Match each item in Column A with an item in Column B. Write the correct letter in each blank. *(10 points each)*

Column A

Column B

_____ **1.** amnesty

A. John Wilkes Booth

_____ **2.** radical

B. Restoration

_____ **3.** assassinated President Abraham Lincoln

C. extreme

_____ **4.** leading Radical Republican

D. pardon

_____ **5.** Andrew Johnson's reconstruction plan

E. Thaddeus Stevens

Short Answer **DIRECTIONS:** Answer each question below in the space provided. *(10 points each)*

6. What was the Ten Percent Plan?

_____

_____

7. Which bill barred former Confederates from holding public office?

_____

_____

8. What 1865 agency helped former enslaved people adjust to freedom?

_____

_____

9. Who was the only Southern senator to support the Union during the Civil War?

_____

10. What did the Thirteenth Amendment to the Constitution do?

_____

_____

Score: _____

Section Quiz 17-2
Radicals in Control

Matching   DIRECTIONS: Match each item in Column A with an item in Column B. Write the correct letter in each blank. *(10 points each)*

Column A

_____ **1.** to defeat a president's veto

_____ **2.** divided Southern states into military districts

_____ **3.** to charge with wrongdoing

_____ **4.** 1868 Republican presidential candidate

_____ **5.** 1868 Democratic presidential candidate

Column B

A. Ulysses S. Grant

B. Horatio Seymour

C. override

D. First Reconstruction Act

E. impeach

Short Answer   DIRECTIONS: Answer each question below in the space provided. *(10 points each)*

6. What were the laws passed by Southern states to prevent African Americans from owning land?

_____

_____

7. What powers did Congress give to the Freedmen's Bureau in 1866?

_____

_____

8. Which amendment excluded Native Americans from citizenship?

_____

9. Why did the House of Representatives vote to impeach Johnson?

_____

_____

10. Who won the presidential election of 1868?

_____

_____

Section Quiz 17-3

The South During Reconstruction

Matching   DIRECTIONS: Match each item in Column A with an item in Column B. Write the correct letter in each blank. *(10 points each)*

Column A

_____ **1.** African American senator

_____ **2.** dishonest or illegal actions

_____ **3.** lent money to help African Americans buy land

_____ **4.** helped with education

_____ **5.** includes whites and African Americans

Column B

A. Freedmen's Bureau

B. Freedmen's Bank

C. integrate

D. corruption

E. Hiram Revels

Short Answer   DIRECTIONS: Answer each question below in the space provided. *(10 points each)*

6. Name the two African Americans who served in the Senate between 1869 and 1880.

_____

7. Who were the carpetbaggers?

_____

_____

8. What group used fear and violence to deny rights to freed men and women?

_____

9. Whom did former Confederates refer to as scalawags?

_____

_____

10. How did the sharecropping system work?

_____

_____

Name_____ Date_____ Class_____

Section Quiz 17-4

Change in the South

Matching   DIRECTIONS: Match each item in Column A with an item in Column B. Write the correct letter in each blank. *(10 points each)*

Column A

_____ **1.** coming together again

_____ **2.** African American civil rights leader

_____ **3.** Horace Greeley's opponent

_____ **4.** terrorized Republican voters

_____ **5.** separation of the races

Column B

A. Ulysses S. Grant

B. Ku Klux Klan

C. W.E.B. Du Bois

D. segregation

E. reconciliation

Short Answer   DIRECTIONS: Answer each question below in the space provided. *(10 points each)*

6. What did the Amnesty Act do?

_____

_____

7. What happened as a result of the Panic of 1873?

_____

8. Who were the Redeemers?

_____

_____

9. What did supporters of a "New South" believe was needed for a strong economy?

_____

_____

10. Name two ways Southern leaders denied African Americans the right to vote.

_____

_____

Chapter 17 Test, Form A
Reconstruction and the New South

Matching **DIRECTIONS:** Match each item in Column A with an item in Column B. Write the correct letter in each blank. *(5 points each)*

Column A

_____ **1.** extreme approach to politics

_____ **2.** crops sold for money

_____ **3.** to defeat a veto

_____ **4.** laws to control freed men and women

_____ **5.** hanging

Column B

A. override

B. lynching

C. black codes

D. cash crops

E. radical

Multiple Choice **DIRECTIONS:** In the blank, write the letter of the choice that best completes the statement or answers the question. *(8 points each)*

_____ **6.** After the Civil War, the period of rebuilding the South was called

    A. Reconstruction.
    B. Reorganization.
    C. Rebuilding.
    D. Reformation.

_____ **7.** The rival plan proposed by Congress to President Abraham Lincoln's Reconstruction plan was the

    A. Rival Bill.
    B. Fifteenth Amendment.
    C. Wade-Davis Bill.
    D. Freedmen's Bureau.

_____ **8.** Northerners who supported the Republicans and moved to the South during Reconstruction were called

    A. scalawags.
    B. carpetbaggers.
    C. freedmen.
    D. fugitives.

_____ **9.** To all white Southerners, except Confederate leaders, Lincoln offered

    A. the Ten Percent Plan.
    B. reconstruction.
    C. freedom.
    D. amnesty.

_____ **10.** Which amendment says that no state could take away a citizen's life, liberty, and property "without due process of law"?

    A. Thirteenth Amendment
    B. Sixteenth Amendment
    C. Fourteenth Amendment
    D. Fifteenth Amendment

Test, Form A (continued)

DBQ **Document-Based Questions** **DIRECTIONS:** Answer the questions in the space provided. (*10 points each*)

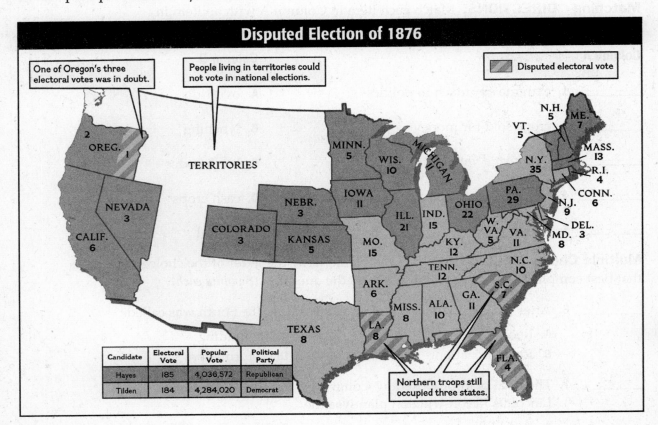

Disputed Election of 1876

One of Oregon's three electoral votes was in doubt.

People living in territories could not vote in national elections.

Disputed electoral vote

Northern troops still occupied three states.

Candidate	Electoral Vote	Popular Vote	Political Party
Hayes	185	4,036,572	Republican
Tilden	184	4,284,020	Democrat

_____ **11.** In which of the following states was the electoral vote of the 1876 election not disputed?

    A. Mississippi   **C.** Florida

    B. Oregon   **D.** Louisiana

_____ **12.** According to the map and chart, who received the most popular votes in the 1876 election?

    A. Grant   **C.** Hayes

    B. Tilden   **D.** Lincoln

Essay **DIRECTIONS:** Answer the following question on a separate sheet of paper. (*15 points*)

13. What was the Fifteenth Amendment, and which U.S. citizens did it affect?

Score: _____

Chapter 17 Test, Form B

Reconstruction and the New South

Matching DIRECTIONS: Match each item in Column A with an item in Column B. Write the correct letter in each blank. *(5 points each)*

Column A

_____ **1.** Radical Republican

_____ **2.** war hero president

_____ **3.** African American senator

_____ **4.** secret society of terrorists

_____ **5.** impeached president

Column B

A. Andrew Johnson

B. Thaddeus Stevens

C. Blanche K. Bruce

D. Ku Klux Klan

E. Ulysses S. Grant

Multiple Choice DIRECTIONS: In the blank, write the letter of the choice that best completes the statement or answers the question. *(8 points each)*

_____ **6.** Who was accused of assassinating President Abraham Lincoln?

    A. Wade Davis

    B. Dr. Samuel Mudd

    C. John Wilkes Booth

    D. William Petersen

_____ **7.** Which amendment grants full citizenship to all individuals born in the United States?

    A. Thirteenth Amendment

    B. Fourteenth Amendment

    C. Fifteenth Amendment

    D. Sixteenth Amendment

_____ **8.** Which agency helped freed African Americans by establishing schools?

    A. Freedmen's Bureau

    B. Wade-Davis Bill

    C. Southerners' Society

    D. Reconstruction Bureau

_____ **9.** When President Andrew Johnson violated the Tenure of Office Act, he was

    A. reelected.

    B. supported.

    C. impeached.

    D. overridden.

_____ **10.** One of the leading industries of the New South was

    A. textiles.

    B. dairy farming.

    C. printing.

    D. music.

Test, Form B (continued)

DBQ **Document-Based Questions** **DIRECTIONS:** Answer the questions in the space provided. (*10 points each*)

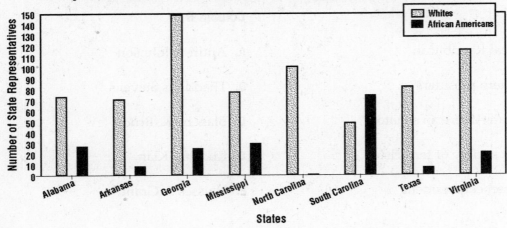

Composition of Lower Houses of State Legislatures, 1870–1871

_____ 11. According to the graph, which state had more African American than white representatives?

   A. Georgia   **C.** South Carolina
   B. North Carolina   **D.** Texas

_____ 12. According to the graph, in which of the following states was African American representation the lowest?

   A. Georgia   **C.** Virginia
   B. South Carolina   **D.** North Carolina

Essay **DIRECTIONS:** Answer the following question on a separate sheet of paper. (*15 points*)

13. What were the black codes, and how did they hurt African Americans?

Score: _____

Chapter 17 Test, Form C

Reconstruction and the New South

Matching   DIRECTIONS: Match each item in Column A with an item in Column B. Write the correct letter in each blank. *(5 points each)*

Column A

_____ **1.** Secretary of War

_____ **2.** civil rights leader

_____ **3.** champion of political reform

_____ **4.** editor of the *Atlanta Constitution*

_____ **5.** African American senator

Column B

A. Edwin Stanton

B. Hiram Revels

C. Rutherford B. Hayes

D. Henry Grady

E. W.E.B. Du Bois

Multiple Choice   DIRECTIONS: In the blank, write the letter of the choice that best completes the statement or answers the question. *(8 points each)*

_____ **6.** What did many freed men and women consider to be slavery in disguise?

    A. slave codes

    B. poll taxes

    C. literacy tests

    D. black codes

_____ **7.** What did Congress pass to prohibit the president from removing government officials without the Senate's approval?

    A. Impeachment Act

    B. black codes

    C. Tenure of Office Act

    D. override

_____ **8.** Northerners who supported the Republicans and moved to the South during Reconstruction were called

    A. scalawags.

    B. carpetbaggers.

    C. freedmen.

    D. fugitives.

_____ **9.** What changed the political balance in the South by restoring full rights to people who supported the Democrats?

    A. Amnesty Act

    B. Freedmen's Bureau

    C. Fifteenth Amendment

    D. Reconstruction Act

_____ **10.** Republicans in Congress easily overrode Johnson's vetoes and took charge of Reconstruction during

    A. Radical Reconstruction.

    B. Restoration.

    C. Congressional Reconstruction.

    D. Radical Rebuilding.

Test, Form C (continued)

DBQ Document-Based Questions **DIRECTIONS:** Answer the questions in the space provided. *(10 points each)*

> "The military rule which [the First Reconstruction Act] establishes is plainly to be used, not for any purpose of order or for the prevention of crime, but solely as a means of coercing the people into the adoption of principles and measures to which it is known that they are opposed, and upon which they have an undeniable right to exercise their own judgment.
>
> "I submit to Congress whether this measure is not in . . . palpable conflict with the plainest provisions of the Constitution, and utterly destructive to those great principles of liberty and humanity for which our ancestors on both sides of the Atlantic have shed so much blood and expended so much treasure. . . ."
>
> —President Andrew Johnson, 1867

_____ **11.** This excerpt from a message to Congress by Johnson argues that the First Reconstruction Act

   A. is a necessary measure to maintain order in the Southern states.

   B. is contrary to the Constitution.

   C. will encourage the Southern states to recover.

   D. will help African Americans.

12. What does Johnson think the First Reconstruction Act would do?

_____

_____

Essay **DIRECTIONS:** Answer the following question on a separate sheet of paper. *(15 points)*

13. Why did the results of the Congressional elections of 1874 weaken Congress's commitment to Reconstruction and support for African American rights?

Answer Key

The First Americans

Section Quiz 1-1

Matching
1. B   3. D   5. A
2. E   4. C

Short Answer
6. Asia
7. wooly mammoths
8. in pursuit of game animals to use for food, tools, and housing
9. Beringia land bridge
10. the development of maize and farming

Section Quiz 1-2

Matching
1. C   3. E   5. D
2. A   4. B

Completion
6. religious rituals
7. hieroglyphics
8. Mexico City
9. quipus
10. terraces

Section Quiz 1-3

Matching
1. D   3. E   5. A
2. C   4. B

Short Answer
6. Utah, Colorado, Arizona, and New Mexico
7. the Inuit
8. stone pyramids built by the Maya and the Aztec
9. adobe
10. the Iroquois; to protect the tribes from destruction and elimination

Chapter 1 Test, Form A

Matching
1. A   3. C   5. B
2. E   4. D

Multiple Choice
6. C   8. B   10. C
7. D   9. D

Document-Based Questions
11. B   12. C

Essay
13. Early peoples probably came from Asia across a land bridge called Beringia, which appeared during the Ice Age due to low sea levels. The bridge linked Siberia to North America. They most likely came in search of food, possibly following the mammoths or other large game.

Chapter 1 Test, Form B

Matching
1. B   3. E   5. D
2. A   4. C

Multiple Choice
6. D   8. B   10. A
7. B   9. D

Document-Based Questions
11. B   12. C

Essay
13. Native peoples used their environment for food, shelter, and clothing. For example, the Hohokam dug irrigation channels to water their fields, and the Anasazi used the native stone and natural cliffs to build housing. The Inuit wore sealskins to protect themselves from the climate. The Plains peoples became skilled riders because there were plenty of horses in their region. The peoples of the Northwest ate salmon as their mainstay.

Answer Key

Chapter 1 Test, Form C

Matching
1. C 3. E 5. D
2. B 4. A

Multiple Choice
6. C 8. C 10. D
7. A 9. A

Document-Based Questions
11. A 12. C

Essay
13. The Iroquois formed the Iroquois League to promote peace. The five nations of the Iroquois League were: Onondaga, Seneca, Mohawk, Oneida, and Cayuga. These nations fought with each other before the Iroquois brought them together in the federation. The Iroquois League was a complex political system for the purpose of governing these nations in peace.

Exploring the Americas

Section Quiz 2-1

Matching
1. D 3. E 5. C
2. A 4. B

Short Answer
6. *Travels*
7. rebirth
8. Europe developed from a group of small states into a new type of centralized state. Strong monarchs came to power in certain countries and sought ways to increase trade in their countries in order to make them stronger.
9. Ghana prospered from the taxes they placed on the things that they traded.
10. the renewed interest in classical Greek and Roman learning

Section Quiz 2-2

Matching
1. C 3. E 5. B
2. D 4. A

Short Answer
6. Portugal lacked a Mediterranean port and could not share in the trade between Asia and Europe. It wanted to find routes to China and India to start trading on its own.
7. A saga is a traditional story.
8. Most educated people believed the earth was round but did not know how large it was. They based their estimates on Ptolemy, who underestimated the size of the world.
9. He planned voyages and analyzed the data brought back by the sailors. He also organized a school for navigation to allow for the sharing of the knowledge gained from each trip.
10. Isabella agreed to sponsor Columbus if he promised to bring Christianity to the lands that he found and she knew if trade opened up with Asia that Spain would become wealthy.

Section Quiz 2-3

Matching
1. B 3. A 5. E
2. D 4. C

Short Answer
6. The Seven Cities of Cibola, or the Seven Cities of Gold, is a tale that was told to explorers who were looking for wealth in their travels. They do not exist, but they did inspire two explorers to travel into what is now the American Southwest.
7. Hernando de Soto
8. He captured their captain, falsely accused him of crimes and executed him. Without their leader the Inca were not able to fight as effectively. Pizarro took over.

Answer Key

9. replacing enslaved Native Americans who were working on plantations with enslaved Africans

10. top: *peninsulares*, second: creoles, third: *mestizos*, fourth: Native Americans, fifth: enslaved Africans

Section Quiz 2-4

Matching
1. E
2. D
3. B
4. A
5. C

Short Answer
6. He rejected many practices because they were not mentioned in the Bible.

7. Because the voyage to Asia was very long and difficult, so they wanted a direct water route through the Americas.

8. The divisions between the Catholics and the Protestants divided the Americas. The Spanish and French spread Catholicism to the areas they settled in, being the southwest and the northeast. The Dutch and the English with Protestantism settled along the Atlantic coast.

9. *Coureurs de bois,* or "runners of the woods"

10. Martin Luther nailed a list of complaints about the Catholic Church on a local church door.

Chapter 2 Test, Form A

Matching
1. D
2. C
3. A
4. E
5. B

Multiple Choice
6. D
7. C
8. D
9. C
10. B

Document-Based Questions
11. C
12. B

Essay
13. The desire to share in the riches of Asia led to European expeditions to find new and better trade routes to Asia. This exploration led to the discovery of lands new to them. For example, Columbus sailed on behalf of Spain in order to find better trade routes, but instead, he discovered America.

Chapter 2 Test, Form B

Matching
1. E
2. C
3. A
4. D
5. B

Multiple Choice
6. B
7. B
8. A
9. C
10. D

Document-Based Questions
11. D
12. B

Essay
13. The Spanish had watched Portugal become wealthy from Asian trade. After the last Muslim kingdom in Spain was driven out in 1492, King Ferdinand and Queen Isabella could focus on their goal of opening a way to Asia. Columbus promised to find a passage and also to bring Christianity to any lands he found.

Chapter 2 Test, Form C

Matching
1. A
2. E
3. B
4. D
5. C

Multiple Choice
6. D
7. B
8. C
9. A
10. A

Document-Based Questions
11. B
12. D

Answer Key

Essay

13. The introduction of the printing press exposed more people to books and information about the world. Better maps and navigation instruments, like the astrolabe and magnetic compass, made sea travel much easier. And, better ships, like the caravel, made long ocean voyages possible.

Colonial America

Section Quiz 3-1

Matching

1. C   3. E   5. D
2. A   4. B

Short Answer

6. Sir Walter Raleigh
7. They had a difficult winter and returned home.
8. 19 years
9. A group of merchants called the Virginia Company of London.
10. They starved and fought with the Native Americans.

Section Quiz 3-2

Matching

1. B   3. A   5. C
2. D   4. E

Short Answer

6. religious freedom
7. Roger Williams
8. No—they had difficulty finding work and they felt that their children were losing their religious values and English way of life.
9. The compact was a document that the colonists created in which they pledged their loyalty to England, and stated their intention of creating a "body politic."

10. Answers may vary but should include: growing corn, beans, and pumpkins; where to hunt and fish.

Section Quiz 3-3

Matching

1. D   3. C   5. A
2. B   4. E

Short Answer

6. It had a strong seaport that caused it to become the center of shipping to and from the Americas.
7. The Quakers
8. The Charter of Liberties
9. New York City
10. Delaware

Section Quiz 3-4

Matching

1. A   3. E   5. B
2. C   4. D

Short Answer

6. No—English criminals and prisoners of war were sent here to earn their freedom through work. Enslaved African prisoners came too.
7. An indentured servant is a person who comes to America and to pay their passage, they agree to work without pay for a certain amount of time.
8. It showed that the new settlers would not be limited to the coast, and that they were going to have to open up more land for settlement.
9. No—instead of a place for debtors to make a new start, hundreds of poor people and refugees came there and settled. They did not like the rules of the colony and complained and so the leader gave up.
10. almost 150 years

Answer Key

Chapter 3 Test, Form A

Matching
1. D
2. A
3. E
4. B
5. C

Multiple Choice
6. C
7. C
8. A
9. B
10. A

Document-Based Questions
11. B
12. C

Essay
13. By the early 1700s, Carolina's settlers wanted political power. In 1719 the southern settlers seized control of the colony from its proprietors. In 1729 Carolina was formally divided into North Carolina and South Carolina.

Chapter 3 Test, Form B

Matching
1. C
2. D
3. A
4. E
5. B

Multiple Choice
6. A
7. B
8. C
9. D
10. D

Document-Based Questions
11. strangers; by 32% or almost half
12. English colonists who were not Pilgrims

Essay
13. Colonists faced severe hardships in the colonies, including cold weather, disease, and malnutrition. Native Americans taught the colonists how to grow crops, hunt, and fish so they could feed themselves. Native Americans also traded with the colonists. Later the colonists needed more land and drove many of the Native Americans off the land.

Chapter 3 Test, Form C

Matching
1. B
2. D
3. E
4. C
5. A

Multiple Choice
6. D
7. A
8. D
9. C
10. B

Document-Based Questions
11. The Pilgrims were a close group who had been persecuted by outsiders. So people who were not Pilgrims were considered to be strangers, rather than friends.
12. 66 days

Essay
13. Pilgrims were Separatists from the Netherlands who wanted to practice their religion freely and they made an arrangement to settle in Virginia. They called themselves Pilgrims because their journey had a religious purpose.

Growth of the Thirteen Colonies

Section Quiz 4-1

Matching
1. D
2. A
3. E
4. B
5. C

Short Answer
6. rice
7. increase in enslaved African Americans, increase in immigration, larger colonial families
8. Answers may vary but should include spinning yarn, preserving fruit, milking cows, fencing in fields, and sowing and harvesting grain.

Answer Key

9. They were strict rules that governed the behavior and punishment of enslaved African Americans.

10. because they restricted trade for the colonists

Section Quiz 4-2

Matching
1. E   3. A   5. D
2. C   4. B

Short Answer
6. William and Mary were the people who replaced James II as rulers of England during the Glorious Revolution.

7. They were viewed as an economic investment.

8. the concept of limited government, protection from unjust punishment, and the protection of life, liberty, and property

9. religion, education, and the arts

10. Zenger's libel case against the *New York Journal*

Section Quiz 4-3

Matching
1. D   3. A   5. B
2. C   4. E

Short Answer
6. the Six Nations

7. none of the colonists agreed to its adoption

8. They had a strong connection through fur trade. The French did not want to take over Native American land. Many French trappers and traders often married Native American women. Finally, many Native Americans converted to Catholicism through French missionaries.

9. Britain and France

10. that the French had already established a fort there

Section Quiz 4-4

Matching
1. B   3. A   5. C
2. D   4. E

Short Answer
6. The struggle was also over control of world trade and power on the seas.

7. It helped to end the possibility of France as a power in North America. Britain and Spain would have it all.

8. The chances of winning the war became greater because Pitt was a great military planner.

9. He warned Braddock that his army's style of marching was not well suited to fighting on the frontier. The lines and the bright colored uniforms made them easy targets.

10. Great Britain would pay for it and then increase the taxes of the colonists to help pay off the debt.

Chapter 4 Test, Form A

Matching
1. E   3. C   5. D
2. B   4. A

Multiple Choice
6. A   8. B   10. D
7. C   9. C

Document-Based Questions
11. B   12. D

Essay
13. The triangular trade was the name of the passage that ships took to exchange goods. The name was given because the trade routes were triangle-shaped. Ships brought sugar and molasses from the West Indies to the New England colonies, where the molasses was made into rum. Rum and other goods were shipped to West Africa and traded for enslaved Africans.

Answer Key

Chapter 4 Test, Form B

Matching
1. D   3. A   5. B
2. C   4. E

Multiple Choice
6. A   8. C   10. D
7. C   9. B

Document-Based Questions
11. A   12. D

Essay
13. The three types of colonies are the charter colonies, proprietary colonies, and royal colonies. Charter colonies include Connecticut and Rhode Island. They were established by a group of settlers who had been given a charter. They elected their own governors and members of the legislature. Although Britain had the right to approve the governor's appointment, the governor could not veto the acts of the legislature. Proprietary colonies were Delaware, Maryland, and Pennsylvania. They were ruled by proprietors who were granted land by Britain. Proprietors were generally free to rule as they wished. Proprietary colonies appointed the governor and members of the upper house of legislature, while the people elected the lower house. Royal colonies were Georgia, Massachusetts, New Hampshire, New Jersey, New York, North Carolina, South Carolina, and Virginia. These were ruled directly by Britain. The king appointed a governor and council, known as the upper house, and the colonists elected an assembly, called the lower house. The governor and members of the council usually did what the British leaders told them to do, which often led to conflict with the assembly.

Chapter 4 Test, Form C

Matching
1. B   3. E   5. A
2. C   4. D

Multiple Choice
6. C   8. A   10. A
7. D   9. D

Document-Based Questions
11. A
12. Answers might vary, but could include the clearing of land and building roads in the forest.

Essay
13. Most New England colonists were English, but a great many settlers in the Middle Colonies were German, Dutch, or Swedish. These different immigrants practiced different religions. The cultural and religious diversity encouraged tolerance for such differences.

The Spirit of Independence

Section Quiz 5-1

Matching
1. C   3. B   5. D
2. E   4. A

Short Answer
6. legal documents that allowed customs officers to enter any location to search for smuggled goods
7. They drafted a petition to the king and Parliament declaring that the colonies could not be taxed except by their own assemblies.
8. prevented the colonists from moving west into the Appalachian territories
9. It created the Declaratory Act which stated that they had the right to tax and make decisions for the colonies.

Answer Key

10. Answers may vary but should include the formation of groups like the Daughters of Liberty; boycotts; urged Americans to wear homemade fabrics and produce other goods that they needed rather than buy British goods.

Section Quiz 5-2

Matching

1. D   3. B   5. A
2. E   4. C

Short Answer

6. It repealed all of the Townsend Acts except the one on tea.

7. the committee of correspondence

8. Answers may very but should include taxes imposed on the colonies, armies sent in to occupy cities, soldiers being rude and violent to colonists, soldiers stealing from shops, fighting with people, and competing for jobs.

9. Closing the harbor blocked off the arrival of food and other supplies that arrived by ship.

10. They felt that the acts violated their rights as English citizens.

Section Quiz 5-3

Matching

1. B   3. E   5. C
2. D   4. A

Short Answer

6. He had instructions to take away the weapons of the militia and arrest the leaders.

7. Captain John Parker

8. These were resolutions that called on the people of the county to arm themselves against the British and form militias.

9. Fort Ticonderoga

10. that the Americans would not be easily defeated

Section Quiz 5-4

Matching

1. E   3. A   5. D
2. C   4. B

Short Answer

6. John Locke

7. John Hancock

8. Answers may vary but can include that people are born with certain rights to life, liberty, and property; they can form governments to protect these rights; and that a government interfering with those rights should be overthrown.

9. July 2, 1776

10. 56

Chapter 5 Test, Form A

Matching

1. A   3. C   5. D
2. E   4. B

Multiple Choice

6. C   8. A   10. B
7. B   9. B

Document-Based Questions

11. D   12. A

Essay

13. The First Continental Congress drafted a statement of grievances calling for the repeal of 13 acts of Parliament passed since 1763. They declared that these laws violated the colonists' rights. The delegates also voted to boycott all British goods and trade, and to arm themselves and form militias.

Chapter 5 Test, Form B

Matching

1. A   3. B   5. C
2. D   4. E

Answer Key

Multiple Choice

6. C	**8.** B	**10.** A
7. A	**9.** C	

Document-Based Questions

11. C   **12.** A

Essay

13. As word of the Boston Tea Party spread through the colonies, the colonists celebrated the Boston Sons of Liberty's act of defiance. No one had yet spoken of challenging British rule, and most colonists still considered themselves British citizens.

Chapter 5 Test, Form C

Matching

1. C	**3.** A	**5.** D
2. B	**4.** E	

Multiple Choice

6. D	**8.** D	**10.** C
7. A	**9.** D	

Document-Based Questions

11. D   **12.** C

Essay

13. The Sugar Act, while unpopular, directly affected fewer people than the Stamp Act did. Because all printed material, from newspapers to wills, had to have a stamp, almost everyone in colonial cities had to pay the stamp tax.

The American Revolution

Section Quiz 6-1

Matching

1. B	**3.** A	**5.** C
2. D	**4.** E	

Short Answer

6. mercenaries and the Hessians

7. He announced that the enslaved people who fought on the British side would be freed.

8. Answers may vary but should include that they did not trust the Continental Congress to protect their liberties; each state pursued its own interests, and faced difficulty enlisting soldiers and raising money to fight.

9. The winter of 1776–1777. They were freezing, starving, and sick. Many soldiers died or deserted.

10. with a 3-pronged attack—Burgoyne coming south from Canada, Leger east from Lake Ontario, and Howe coming north from New York City. The three would meet at Albany.

Section Quiz 6-2

Matching

1. E	**3.** C	**5.** B
2. D	**4.** A	

Short Answer

6. Valley Forge

7. He drilled the troops and taught them military discipline.

8. The bills lost value because the circulation grew faster than the supply of gold and silver backing them.

9. Judith Sargeant Murray

10. Answers may vary but should include that they fled the colonies, they were shunned by neighbors, they were victims of violence, they were arrested and tried as traitors, and some were even executed.

Section Quiz 6-3

Matching

1. C	**3.** A	**5.** D
2. E	**4.** B	

Answer Key

Short Answer

6. the capture of Charles Town

7. A privateer is a merchant ship that is privately owned and has weapons.

8. Henry Hamilton because he paid for settlers' scalps

9. He organized troops and marched on the British posts set up along the Mississippi River. His victories opened supply lines for military goods.

10. He carried out raids throughout the state and almost captured Jefferson and the Virginia legislature.

Section Quiz 6-4

Matching

1. B   3. C   5. E
2. D   4. A

Short Answer

6. Yes—the British were trapped by the American and French troops and could not escape by sea.

7. Benjamin Franklin, John Adams, and John Jay

8. Lafayette would keep them bottled up on the peninsula, Admiral de Grasse would trap them using the bay, and Washington would keep his plans a secret to prevent Clinton from sending aid.

9. Answers may vary but should include that the United States was recognized as an independent nation; the withdrawal of British troops from American territory; and the Americans had the right to fish the waters off the coast of Canada.

10. It was a people's movement—it was not based on one battle but the determination and spirit of a people.

Chapter 6 Test, Form A

Matching

1. A   3. C   5. D
2. E   4. B

Multiple Choice

6. C   8. B   10. C
7. A   9. C

Document-Based Questions

11. D   12. hostile

Essay

13. Other nations that helped the Americans win the war included France and Spain. The French worked out a trade agreement and an alliance. France declared war on Britain and sent money, equipment, and troops to aid the Americans. Spain also declared war on Britain. The Spanish governor of Louisiana raised an army and forced British troops out. Spanish troops captured British forts in the South. European nations helped the American cause mostly because they hated the British.

Chapter 6 Test, Form B

Matching

1. E   3. D   5. B
2. C   4. A

Multiple Choice

6. B   8. B   10. D
7. D   9. C

Document-Based Questions

11. Savannah, Charles Town, and Camden

12. Yorktown

Essay

13. The American army consisted mostly of American colonists, while the British army contained many Hessian mercenaries. While the American colonists were fighting on their own soil for their country's freedom, the mercenaries in the British army had no personal stake in the outcome, and were fighting only for money.

Answer Key

Chapter 6 Test, Form C

Matching
1. D   3. A   5. E
2. B   4. C

Multiple Choice
6. C   8. A   10. D
7. B   9. B

Document-Based Questions
11. D   12. C

Essay
13. To pay for the war, Congress and the states printed hundreds of millions of dollars worth of paper money. These bills quickly lost their value, however, because the amount of bills in circulation grew faster than the supply of gold and silver backing them. This situation led to inflation, which means that it took more and more money to buy the same amount of goods.

A More Perfect Union

Section Quiz 7-1

Matching
1. B   3. A   5. D
2. E   4. C

Short Answer
6. their experience with British rule
7. Americans won their independence, expanded foreign trade, and aided with the settling of Western territories.
8. the Northwest Ordinance
9. a 5 percent tax on imported goods
10. They claimed the Americans had failed to honor their promises made in the same treaty.

Section Quiz 7-2

Matching
1. D   3. A   5. B
2. E   4. C

Short Answer
6. They felt it was too weak to deal with the problems of a new nation.
7. They worried that the government could not control unrest and prevent violence.
8. James Madison
9. an agreement between two or more sides in which each side gives up some of what it wants
10. a bill of rights

Section Quiz 7-3

Matching
1. C   3. D   5. B
2. A   4. E

Short Answer
6. to avoid the mistakes of the past
7. sharing power between federal and state governments
8. the legislative branch
9. to describe each branch of government's powers and responsibilities
10. It lacked a bill of rights to protect individual freedoms.

Chapter 7 Test, Form A

Matching
1. C   3. A   5. B
2. E   4. D

Multiple Choice
6. B   8. C   10. B
7. C   9. A

Answer Key

Document-Based Questions
11. Virginia; 292,627

12. New Hampshire; 157

Essay
13. Part of the Great Compromise addressed how enslaved persons were to be counted in a state's population. Southern states wanted to include enslaved Africans in their population count to gain delegates in the House of Representatives. Northern states objected to this idea because enslaved people were legally considered property. Some delegates from Northern states argued that enslaved laborers, as property, should be counted for the purpose of taxation but not representation. However, neither side considered giving enslaved African Americans the right to vote. The committee's solution was to count each enslaved person as three-fifths of a free person for both taxation and representation, which became known as Three-Fifths Compromise.

Chapter 7 Test, Form B

Matching
1. D	**3.** E	**5.** C
2. B	**4.** A	

Multiple Choice
6. A	**8.** B	**10.** C
7. B	**9.** C	

Document-Based Questions
11. A   **12.** A

Essay
13. The legislative branch is the lawmaking branch of the government composed of the House of Representatives and the Senate; the powers of Congress include collecting taxes, coining money, and regulating trade; Congress can declare war and "raise and support armies;" it can also make all laws needed to fulfill the functions given to it by the Constitution. The executive branch is headed by the president to carry out the nation's laws and policies; the president serves as the commander in chief of the armed forces and conducts relations with foreign countries. The judicial branch is the court system of the United States, which includes the Supreme Court and any other lower federal courts that Congress might establish; the Supreme Court and the other federal courts hear cases involving the Constitution, laws passed by Congress, and disputes between states.

Chapter 7 Test, Form C

Matching
1. B	**3.** A	**5.** D
2. E	**4.** C	

Multiple Choice
6. C	**8.** C	**10.** D
7. D	**9.** B	

Document-Based Questions
11. B   **12.** C

Essay
13. Slavery was an economic issue as well as a moral issue. Slavery existed in the North, but it was not a major source of labor and many groups worked to end it. The plantation system of the South had been built using enslaved people, and many Southerners feared that their economy could not survive without slavery. Slavery divided the states on the critical issue of whether people should be allowed to enslave other people.

Answer Key

The Federalist Era

Section Quiz 8-1

Matching
1. C   3. A   5. D
2. E   4. B

Short Answer
6. a tax on imports
7. the cabinet
8. Thomas Jefferson
9. with the Judiciary Act of 1789
10. a person who risks money in order to make a profit

Section Quiz 8-2

Matching
1. B   3. A   5. C
2. D   4. E

Short Answer
6. the Whiskey Rebellion; taxes on whiskey
7. General Arthur St. Clair
8. Shawnee chief Blue Jacket
9. free navigation of the Mississippi River and the right to trade at New Orleans
10. It did not deal with the issue of impressments or British interference with American trade.

Section Quiz 8-3

Matching
1. E   3. B   5. D
2. C   4. A

Short Answer
6. He feared they would divide the nation.
7. the Federalists and the Republicans
8. X, Y, and Z
9. immigrants living in the country who are not citizens

10. the Alien and Sedition Acts violated the Constitution

Chapter 8 Test, Form A

Matching
1. C   3. B   5. D
2. E   4. A

Multiple Choice
6. B   8. B   10. A
7. B   9. B

Document-Based Questions
11. B   12. A

Essay
13. With the Judiciary Act of 1789, Congress established a federal court system with 13 district courts and three circuit courts in the nation. State laws would remain, but the federal courts would have the power to reverse state decisions.

Chapter 8 Test, Form B

Matching
1. D   3. A   5. C
2. B   4. E

Multiple Choice
6. C   8. A   10. C
7. A   9. A

Document-Based Questions
11. 53 years old
12. Abigail Adams; 4 years

Essay
13. The Bill of Rights was added to the Constitution because it was believed that a written guarantee of people's liberties was needed. The Bill of Rights limits the power of government. Among other liberties, it protects the people's right to free speech, freedom of religion and assembly, and specifies the rights of

Answer Key

individuals accused of crimes. The Bill of Rights provides the people's check on the power of government.

Chapter 8 Test, Form C

Matching

1. D
3. B
5. A
2. E
4. C

Multiple Choice

6. A
8. C
10. C
7. D
9. A

Document-Based Questions

11. A
12. A

Essay

13. In 1797 it was possible to elect a president and vice president from different parties because, under the provisions of the Constitution, the person with the second highest number of electoral votes became vice president, even though he might represent a different party than the elected president.

The Jefferson Era

Section Quiz 9-1

Matching

1. D
3. E
5. C
2. A
4. B

Short Answer

6. Candidates sent hundreds of letters to leading citizens and newspapers to make their views public.

7. Thomas Jefferson and Aaron Burr

8. After 35 ballots, Alexander Hamilton convinced one of the Federalists not to vote for Burr. Jefferson became president, and Burr became vice president.

9. "Let the people do as they choose."

10. It set up regional courts for the United States, with 16 judges and other judicial officials.

Section Quiz 9-2

Matching

1. C
3. B
5. E
2. D
4. A

Short Answer

6. Spain

7. In 1802 Spain secretly transferred the Louisiana Territory to France.

8. $15 million

9. Both were well-informed amateur scientists, and both had conducted business with Native Americans.

10. Many Federalists opposed the purchase because they feared any new states created from the territory would be Republican. A group of Federalists in Massachusetts plotted to secede from the Union.

Section Quiz 9-3

Matching

1. B
3. E
5. C
2. D
4. A

Short Answer

6. Many French and British merchant ships remained at home to avoid being destroyed or captured by enemy ships. This allowed American shippers to increase trade.

7. Tripoli

8. The British warship, the *Leopard*, fired upon the American ship, *Chesapeake*, killing three crew members.

9. Tecumseh

10. Henry Clay and John Calhoun

Answer Key

Section Quiz 9-4

Matching
1. E   3. A   5. B
2. D   4. C

Short Answer
6. July
7. Oliver Hazard Perry
8. Native Americans
9. the Capitol and the president's mansion
10. the Treaty of Ghent

Chapter 9 Test, Form A

Matching
1. A   3. B   5. C
2. E   4. D

Multiple Choice
6. C   8. C   10. C
7. A   9. D

Document-Based Questions
11. 24 years old; 58 years old
12. 1801

Essay
13. Francis Scott Key, a young attorney, watched as the bombs burst over Fort McHenry in the War of 1812. Finally, "by the dawn's early light," Key was able to see that the American flag still flew over the fort. Deeply moved by patriotic feelings, he wrote a poem called "The Star-Spangled Banner."

Chapter 9 Test, Form B

Matching
1. B   3. D   5. E
2. C   4. A

Multiple Choice
6. B   8. B   10. B
7. B   9. A

Document-Based Questions
11. C   12. B

Essay
13. In 1800 neither John Adams nor Thomas Jefferson traveled around the country making speeches about why he should be elected, the way politicians do today. To do so would have been considered in bad taste. Instead, the candidates and their allies wrote hundreds of letters to leading citizens and friendly newspapers to publicize their views. Students might also mention that there were no televisions and televised campaigns and debates in the election of 1800.

Chapter 9 Test, Form C

Matching
1. A   3. E   5. C
2. D   4. B

Multiple Choice
6. D   8. C   10. C
7. A   9. D

Document-Based Questions
11. Answers will vary, but should include the idea that Jefferson worked his whole life to benefit the people of the United States.
12. U.S. secretary of state

Essay
13. The first principle is the idea that the Constitution is the supreme law of the land. The second principle requires that all laws agree with the Constitution. If there is a conflict between another law and the Constitution, the Constitution must be followed. The third principle

Answer Key

establishes that the judicial branch takes on the role of upholding the Constitution. The judicial branch may nullify all laws determined to be unconstitutional.

Growth and Expansion

Section Quiz 10-1

Matching
1. C
2. A
3. E
4. B
5. D

Short Answer
6. around 1800
7. He memorized the design of the machines he had used in a British factory and duplicated them in a cotton mill in Pawtucket, Rhode Island.
8. capitalism
9. low taxes, minimum government regulations, and competition
10. A patent gives an inventor sole legal right to the invention and its profits for a certain period of time.

Section Quiz 10-2

Matching
1. D
2. C
3. B
4. E
5. A

Short Answer
6. nearly 4 million
7. It viewed the National Road as a military necessity, but didn't take on any other road-building projects.
8. 32 hours; 4 days
9. Teams of mules or horses hauled the boats and barges.
10. nine

Section Quiz 10-3

Matching
1. B
2. E
3. A
4. C
5. D

Short Answer
6. the absence of major political divisions
7. the idea that states have the right to govern themselves
8. The Great Compromiser
9. Spain
10. any future colonization of North and South America by European powers

Chapter 10 Test, Form A

Matching
1. D
2. B
3. E
4. A
5. C

Multiple Choice
6. C
7. C
8. C
9. B
10. B

Document-Based Questions
11. better roads, canals
12. Raw materials could easily get to the North and the East.

Essay
13. Sectionalism, or loyalty to a region, brought an end to the Era of Good Feelings, the period of national harmony. The regional differences became intense as differences arose over national politics. The conflict over slavery divided Northerners, who opposed slavery, and Southerners, who believed in the necessity of slavery. The different regions also disagreed on the need for tariffs, a national bank, and internal improvements, such as canals and roads, to develop the nation's transportation system.

Answer Key

Chapter 10 Test, Form B

Matching
1. B   3. E   5. A
2. C   4. D

Multiple Choice
6. C   8. C   10. D
7. A   9. A

Document-Based Questions
11. C   12. D

Essay
13. There were several significant inventions during the late 1700s and early 1800s that made the Industrial Revolution possible. Among them were the spinning jenny, the water frame, the power loom, and the cotton gin. Each of these inventions improved the way cotton was processed and utilized, saving time and money. Also, Eli Whitney's use of interchangeable parts reduced the price of goods.

Chapter 10 Test, Form C

Matching
1. D   3. E   5. C
2. A   4. B

Multiple Choice
6. C   8. D   10. A
7. A   9. A

Document-Based Questions
11. because the proposal was designed to benefit the whole country
12. Raw materials would be shipped from the South and the West, and manufactured in the East and the North.

Essay
13. James Monroe may have been reelected because he was an experienced politician, having been involved in national politics since the American Revolution. He was a man of dignity who represented a united country free of political strife. Monroe was an unassuming man who toured the nation at his own expense.

The Jackson Era

Section Quiz 11-1

Matching
1. E   3. D   5. B
2. A   4. C

Short Answer
6. National Republicans
7. the spoils system
8. nominating conventions
9. tariffs
10. Force Bill

Section Quiz 11-2

Matching
1. E   3. C   5. D
2. A   4. B

Short Answer
6. Indian Removal Act
7. the Cherokee
8. decided to go to war
9. the Trail of Tears
10. The Seminole

Section Quiz 11-3

Matching
1. D   3. B   5. E
2. A   4. C

Short Answer
6. Nicholas Biddle
7. *McCulloch* v. *Maryland* (1819)

Answer Key

8. He ordered the withdrawal of all government deposits from the Bank and placed the funds in smaller state banks.
9. Land values dropped sharply, investments declined, and banks failed.
10. an independent federal treasury

Chapter 11 Test, Form A

Matching
1. D
2. A
3. E
4. B
5. C

Multiple Choice
6. B
7. C
8. B
9. B
10. A

Document-Based Questions
11. the North and the East
12. the South and the West

Essay
13. In the 1824 election, no candidate received a majority of electoral votes, so the House of Representatives would select the president. Henry Clay, Speaker of the House, agreed to use his influence to help Adams become president. Once in office, Adams appointed Clay secretary of state, traditionally the stepping-stone to the presidency. Andrew Jackson's followers accused the two of making a "corrupt bargain" and stealing the election.

Chapter 11 Test, Form B

Matching
1. D
2. C
3. A
4. E
5. B

Multiple Choice
6. C
7. D
8. C
9. C
10. C

Document-Based Questions
11. B
12. D

Essay
13. The Cherokee Nation refused to give up its land in Georgia and relocate to Indian Territory in Oklahoma. In the treaties of the 1790s, the federal government had recognized the Cherokee people in the state of Georgia as a separate nation with its own laws. Georgia, however, refused to recognize Cherokee laws. The Cherokee sued the state government and eventually took their case to the Supreme Court—*Worcester* v. *Georgia*. Chief Justice John Marshall ruled that Georgia had no right to interfere with the Cherokee because only the federal government had authority over matters concerning the Cherokee. President Jackson supported Georgia's efforts to remove the Cherokee. He vowed to ignore the Supreme Court's ruling.

Chapter 11 Test, Form C

Matching
1. C
2. E
3. B
4. A
5. D

Multiple Choice
6. A
7. B
8. C
9. B
10. C

Document-Based Questions
11. B
12. C

Essay
13. Manufacturers—mostly in the Northeast—welcomed the tariff because tariffs made European goods more expensive, which caused American consumers to buy more American-made products. Southerners, however, were against the tariff because they traded cotton to Europe for manufactured goods, and the tariff made these items more expensive.

Answer Key

Manifest Destiny

Section Quiz 12-1

Matching

1. E   3. B   5. D
2. A   4. C

Short Answer

6. Spain, Great Britain, and Russia
7. fur traders, also known as mountain men
8. the Cayuse
9. Missouri
10. the line of latitude they believed should be the nation's northern border with Oregon

Section Quiz 12-2

Matching

1. C   3. E   5. B
2. A   4. D

Short Answer

6. They had to agree to learn Spanish, become citizens of Mexico, convert to Catholicism, and obey Mexican law.
7. people who obtained land grants and recruited settlers and recruited settlers
8. a decree that stopped all immigration from the United States but encouraged Mexican and European immigrants with generous land grants
9. 12 days
10. Texas allowed slavery and would upset the balance of slave and free states in Congress if admitted to the Union.

Section Quiz 12-3

Matching

1. C   3. E   5. D
2. A   4. B

Short Answer

6. the Santa Fe Trail
7. The nation's border would be the Pacific Ocean instead of land owned by a foreign country, and ports could be built for trade with Asia.
8. $30 million
9. the Mexicans who lived in California
10. Mexico gave up Texas and agreed to the Rio Grande being the border between Texas and Mexico.

Section Quiz 12-4

Matching

1. D   3. B   5. C
2. A   4. E

Short Answer

6. It established a group of reviewers who examined the Californios' land rights.
7. He was the leader of the Mormons and he led them from Illinois to the Great Salt Lake.
8. 1850
9. from translating the words on golden plates given to him by an angel
10. the migration of about 12,000 Mormons to the Great Salt Lake in present-day Utah

Chapter 12 Test, Form A

Matching

1. D   3. C   5. B
2. E   4. A

Multiple Choice

6. D   8. A   10. A
7. D   9. B

Document-Based Questions

11. Democrats
12. Massachusetts

Answer Key

Essay
13. Forty-niners were people looking for gold who arrived in California in 1849.

Chapter 12 Test, Form B

Matching
1. A   **3.** E   **5.** D
2. C   **4.** B

Multiple Choice
6. B   **8.** B   **10.** D
7. A   **9.** A

Document-Based Questions
11. B   **12.** A

Essay
13. President James K. Polk wanted to provoke Mexico into taking military action first. This way, he could justify the war to Congress and the American people. Polk ordered General Zachary Taylor and his troops to the disputed borderland between the Nueces River and the Rio Grande, where they built a fort. A month later, Mexican soldiers attacked a small force of Taylor's soldiers. Polk used this attack as the reason to declare war on Mexico.

Chapter 12 Test, Form C

Matching
1. E   **3.** A   **5.** B
2. D   **4.** C

Multiple Choice
6. C   **8.** C   **10.** A
7. A   **9.** D

Document-Based Questions
11. B
12. Up to this time, American Indians have been forced from their lands and were at odds with whites. This excerpt shows that in some areas and within some groups,

whites and Native Americans were at peace, had trade contracts, and even friendships.

Essay
13. The Oregon Trail and the Santa Fe Trail, forged by the early settlers, opened up the West and made it easier for prospectors and merchants to come to California territory during the Gold Rush.

North and South

Section Quiz 13-1

Matching
1. C   **3.** A   **5.** D
2. E   **4.** B

Short Answer
6. industry, travel, and communications
7. factories
8. canals
9. the mechanical reaper
10. Samuel Morse

Section Quiz 13-2

Matching
1. D   **3.** E   **5.** B
2. A   **4.** C

Short Answer
6. on-the-job accidents
7. an organization of workers with the same trade, or skill
8. The potato crop in Ireland was destroyed by a potato blight, resulting in a severe famine. More than 1.5 million Irish immigrants arrived in the United States during this time.
9. Massachusetts
10. Catholics

Answer Key

Section Quiz 13-3

Matching
1. E
3. D
5. C
2. A
4. B

Short Answer
6. along the Atlantic coast in Maryland, Virginia, and North Carolina
7. a machine that removed cotton seeds from cotton fibers
8. because of their key role in producing cotton and sugar
9. The cotton gin was a machine that removed seeds from cotton fibers. It could clean 50 times more cotton than a person each day, increasing production.
10. They felt the South was too dependent on the North for manufactured goods, and that factories would help the economy of the Upper South.

Section Quiz 13-4

Matching
1. C
3. E
5. D
2. A
4. B

Short Answer
6. fewer than 10
7. slave trade
8. fixed costs
9. the slave codes
10. The South had few people per square mile. Many families could not send their children great distances to attend school. In addition, many Southerners believed education was a private matter, not a state function.

Chapter 13 Test, Form A

Matching
1. B
3. A
5. D
2. C
4. E

Multiple Choice
6. A
8. B
10. C
7. C
9. D

Document-Based Questions
11. horsecar
12. cable car

Essay
13. More enslaved workers enabled Southern cotton growers to increase cotton production.

Chapter 13 Test, Form B

Matching
1. A
3. E
5. C
2. D
4. B

Multiple Choice
6. C
8. D
10. B
7. B
9. A

Document-Based Questions
11. A
12. C

Essay
13. Because farming was so profitable with the boom in cotton, Southern farmers remained committed to farming, rather than starting new businesses. Another stumbling block was the lack of capital to invest in businesses. Wealthy Southerners had their wealth invested in land and slaves. Planters would have had to sell slaves to raise the money to build factories. In addition, the market for manufactured goods in the South was smaller than it was in the North because a large portion of the Southern population consisted of enslaved people with no money to buy merchandise. Also, some Southerners simply did not want industry to flourish there.

Answer Key

Chapter 13 Test, Form C

Matching
1. A   3. E   5. B
2. D   4. C

Multiple Choice
6. B   8. B   10. C
7. C   9. C

Document-Based Questions
11. Clipper ships were powered by wind in sails, steamboats by steam engines. Clipper ships were for ocean travel, steamboats for inland waterways.
12. Horsecars ran on rails; omnibuses did not.

Essay
13. Students may cite any of the following examples: In 1821 New York eliminated the requirement that white men had to own property in order to vote, yet few African Americans were allowed to vote. Both Rhode Island and Pennsylvania passed laws prohibiting free African Americans from voting. Most communities would not allow free African Americans to attend public schools and barred them from public facilities as well. Often African Americans were forced into segregated schools and hospitals.

The Age of Reform

Section Quiz 14-1

Matching
1. C   3. E   5. D
2. A   4. B

Short Answer
6. Oberlin College of Ohio
7. nonviolent refusal to obey laws that are considered unjust
8. the visually impaired
9. the relationship between humans and nature and the importance of individual conscience
10. drinking little or no alcohol

Section Quiz 14-2

Matching
1. D   3. A   5. B
2. E   4. C

Short Answer
6. It did not stop the growth of slavery, and most African Americans did not want to go to Africa. They simply wanted to be free in American society.
7. Sarah and Angelina Grimké
8. the Underground Railroad
9. Elijah Lovejoy
10. reformers who worked to end slavery

Section Quiz 14-3

Matching
1. E   3. B   5. D
2. A   4. C

Short Answer
6. 1920
7. a Declaration of Sentiments and Resolutions
8. Susan B. Anthony
9. Mount Holyoke Female Seminary
10. Wyoming

Chapter 14 Test, Form A

Matching
1. E   3. D   5. A
2. B   4. C

Multiple Choice
6. C   8. B   10. C
7. A   9. C

Answer Key

Document-Based Questions
11. 2

12. Nathaniel Hawthorne, Herman Melville, Edgar Allan Poe, Harriet Beecher Stowe

Essay
13. Several states recognized the right of women to own property after their marriage. Some states passed laws permitting divorced women to share the guardianship of their children with their former husbands. Also, Indiana was the first state to allow women to seek divorce if their husbands were chronic abusers of alcohol.

Chapter 14 Test, Form B

Matching
1. B	**3.** C	**5.** A
2. E	**4.** D	

Multiple Choice
6. B	**8.** B	**10.** D
7. B	**9.** A	

Document-Based Questions
11. C   **12.** A

Essay
13. Writers, such as Thoreau and Emerson, popularized transcendentalism, which urged people to overcome prejudice. Harriet Beecher Stowe brought popular attention to the abolitionist cause and the horrors of slavery with her best seller *Uncle Tom's Cabin*.

Chapter 14 Test, Form C

Matching
1. A	**3.** C	**5.** B
2. D	**4.** E	

Multiple Choice
6. D	**8.** C	**10.** B
7. D	**9.** C	

Document-Based Questions
11. C

12. Girls were usually excluded because many parents thought education was wasted on future wives and mothers. Many African Americans were excluded due to segregation laws. Also many people opposed required education, believing it should be done at home.

Essay
13. The American Colonization Society was the first large-scale antislavery effort aimed at resettling African Americans in Africa or the Caribbean. Formed in 1816 by a group of white Virginians, the society freed enslaved workers by buying them from slaveholders and sending them abroad to start new lives. The problem with the society was that the number of enslaved people continued to increase at a steady pace, and the society could only resettle a small number of people. Furthermore, most African Americans did not want to go to Africa. Many were from families that had lived in the United States for several generations. They simply wanted to be free in American society. African Americans feared that the society might actually strengthen slavery.

Toward Civil War

Section Quiz 15-1

Matching
1. B	**3.** E	**5.** D
2. A	**4.** C	

SHORT ANSWER
6. Congress had eleven of each type of state, with two Senators from each state, making the balance equal.

7. Maine

8. a proposal that would ban slavery in any lands acquired from Mexico

Answer Key

9. "Free Soil, Free Speech, Free Labor, and Free Men"
10. Slave trade was banned, but not slavery itself.

Section Quiz 15-2

Matching
1. E
2. A
3. D
4. B
5. C

Short Answer
6. It convinced more people in the North of the evils of slavery.
7. Henry David Thoreau
8. border ruffians
9. They refused to accept the laws, armed themselves, and adopted their own separate government.
10. Slavery supporters attacked the town, burning the Free State Hotel, and destroying two newspaper offices and many homes.

Section Quiz 15-3

Matching
1. D
2. A
3. E
4. B
5. C

Short Answer
6. Antislavery Whigs and Democrats joined with Free-Soilers.
7. John C. Fremont, James Buchanan, and Millard Fillmore
8. because he had lived in areas of the North where slavery was prohibited
9. Roger B. Taney
10. He hoped to arm enslaved African Americans and start a revolt against slaveholders.

Section Quiz 15-4

Matching
1. B
2. D
3. A
4. E
5. C

Short Answer
6. 4
7. The North was more populous and outvoted the South.
8. slave revolts
9. The Confederate States of America
10. Jefferson Davis sent forces to attack Fort Sumter.

Chapter 15 Test, Form A

Matching
1. E
2. A
3. B
4. C
5. D

Multiple Choice
6. B
7. D
8. A
9. C
10. C

Document-Based Questions
11. Lincoln
12. Douglas

Essay
13. The Missouri Compromise proposed that slavery be prohibited from any territory acquired in the Louisiana Purchase that was north of 36°30'N latitude—except Missouri. Congress would admit Missouri as a slave state and Maine as a free state. This would preserve the balance between slave states and free states in the Senate.

Chapter 15 Test, Form B

Matching
1. B
2. C
3. A
4. E
5. D

Answer Key

Multiple Choice

6. B   8. A   10. C

7. D   9. B

Document-Based Questions

11. D

12. A

Essay

13. The North and the South, with their different economic systems, were competing for new lands in the Western territories. At the same time, a growing number of Northerners wanted to restrict slavery. Even the Southerners who disliked slavery resented Northern interference in their affairs. These differences between the North and the South grew into sectionalism, and this exaggerated loyalty to a particular region split the country.

Chapter 15 Test, Form C

Matching

1. E   3. D   5. C

2. A   4. B

Multiple Choice

6. C   8. C   10. D

7. B   9. A

Document-Based Questions

11. Lincoln won because he still got more votes than any other candidate.

12. slavery

Essay

13. The Compromise of 1820 had prohibited slavery in territories north of 36°30′N that were carved out of the Louisiana Territory, including Kansas and Nebraska. Popular sovereignty would have permitted slavery in those territories as long as the people who lived there voted to allow it.

The Civil War

Section Quiz 16-1

Matching

1. D   3. A   5. B

2. E   4. C

Short Answer

6. It was close to Richmond, the Confederate capital, and Washington, D.C., was within the state. If Maryland seceded, the Union government would be surrounded.

7. to attack Washington, D.C.

8. Winfield Scott

9. the Anaconda Plan

10. 1 of every 8

Section Quiz 16-2

Matching

1. B   3. A   5. D

2. C   4. E

Short Answer

6. David Farragut

7. so they could prevent Louisiana, Arkansas, and Texas from supplying the rest of the Confederacy

8. the Union

9. the right to take property from an enemy in wartime

10. a decree freeing all enslaved people in rebel territory on January 1, 1863

Section Quiz 16-3

Matching

1. E   3. A   5. D

2. C   4. B

Short Answer

6. food, supplies, and even household items

7. nurses and spies

Answer Key

8. Soldiers were crowded together in army camps and drinking from unsanitary water supplies.

9. The Copperheads were the Peace Democrats. Mostly from Ohio, Indiana, and Illinois, they argued for an immediate end to fighting and reuniting the states through negotiation.

10. to end separation of different races and bring equal membership into society

Section Quiz 16-4

Matching
1. B
3. A
5. D
2. E
4. C

Short Answer
6. One of the Confederate companies fired on Jackson's company by mistake. He was wounded in the left arm, which had to be amputated. He died a week later.

7. He failed to obey Lincoln's order to follow the Confederate troops retreating from Antietam and "destroy the rebel army."

8. It pardoned most former Confederates, and nearly all white Southerners could vote and hold office again.

9. two ironclad ships

10. 47 days

Section Quiz 16-5

Matching
1. E
3. A
5. D
2. C
4. B

Short Answer
6. General William Sherman

7. It was a railroad center that was vital for moving troops and supplies. If Petersburg could be taken, then the capital of Richmond would be cut off from the rest of the Confederacy.

8. William T. Sherman's capture of Atlanta

9. Confederate president Davis and his cabinet gathered documents, gave orders to burn bridges and weapons useful to the enemy, and fled Richmond.

10. the era after the Civil War of answering the questions of how to bring the South back into the Union and what the status of African Americans in society would be

Chapter 16 Test, Form A

Matching
1. D
3. C
5. B
2. A
4. E

Multiple Choice
6. B
8. C
10. C
7. D
9. A

Document-Based Questions
11. B
12. C

Essay
13. It would not have changed the enslaved worker's life. The Emancipation Proclamation freed enslaved laborers only in the Confederacy. Because Maryland was in the Union, any enslaved African American living there would have remained in slavery.

Chapter 16 Test, Form B

Matching
1. E
3. C
5. D
2. B
4. A

Multiple Choice
6. D
8. B
10. C
7. A
9. A

Document-Based Questions
11. C
12. panic/fear

Essay
13. Four states that allowed slavery—Missouri, Kentucky, Maryland, and

Answer Key

Delaware—were divided over whether to support the Union or join the Confederacy. Losing these states would damage the North because all had strategic locations. Missouri could control parts of the Mississippi River and major routes to the West. Kentucky controlled the Ohio River. Delaware was close to the important Northern city of Philadelphia. Maryland was close to Richmond, Virginia. Most significantly, Washington, D.C., lay within the state. If Maryland seceded, the North's government would be surrounded.

Chapter 16 Test, Form C

Matching
1. B   3. D   5. E
2. A   4. C

Multiple Choice
6. A   8. C   10. D
7. D   9. B

Document-Based Questions
11. D
12. Lunt is angry and anxious. The Yankees have taken or destroyed everything as they move through the South. The civilians left behind have nothing to eat and all of their basic belongings such as blankets and clothes have been taken.

Essay
13. Although Lincoln hated slavery, he was at first reluctant to move against it because of the border states. Northerners like Horace Greely and Frederick Douglass made several arguments to support ending slavery. They pointed out that it was morally wrong, that it was the root of the division between North and South, and casting the war as a fight for freedom would convince antislavery nations like Britain and France not to support the Confederates.

Reconstruction and the New South

Section Quiz 17-1

Matching
1. D   3. A   5. B
2. C   4. E

Short Answer
6. It was Lincoln's plan for accepting Southern states back into the Union. If 10 percent of the voters of a state took an oath of loyalty to the Union, that state could form a new government and adopt a new constitution that banned slavery.
7. the Wade-Davis Bill
8. the Freedmen's Bureau
9. Andrew Johnson
10. It abolished slavery throughout the United States.

Section Quiz 17-2

Matching
1. C   3. E   5. B
2. D   4. A

Short Answer
6. the black codes
7. the power to try individuals charged with violating the rights of African Americans
8. the Fourteenth Amendment
9. They were outraged because he violated the Tenure of Office Act by removing Secretary of War Edwin Stanton from office.
10. Ulysses S. Grant

Section Quiz 17-3

Matching
1. E   3. B   5. C
2. D   4. A

Answer Key

Short Answer
6. Hiram Revels and Blanche K. Bruce
7. Northerners who moved to the South after the war. Although some were dishonest, most were not. Many were reformers who wanted to help the South.
8. the Ku Klux Klan
9. Southern whites who backed the Republicans
10. A landowner rented a plot of land to a farmer, along with seeds and tools, a mule, and a crude shack. In return, sharecroppers shared a percentage of their crop with the landowner.

Section Quiz 17-4

Matching
1. E
3. A
5. D
2. C
4. B

Short Answer
6. pardoned most former Confederates
7. Small banks were forced to close, the stock market plummeted, thousands of businesses closed, and tens of thousands of Americans were thrown out of work.
8. Democrats who saved the South from Republican rule
9. They believed the New South should have industry founded on the region's abundance of coal, iron, tobacco, cotton, and lumber.
10. poll taxes and literacy tests

Chapter 17 Test, Form A

Matching
1. E
3. A
5. B
2. D
4. C

Multiple Choice
6. A
8. B
10. C
7. C
9. D

Document-Based Questions
11. A
12. B

Essay
13. The Fifteenth Amendment prohibited the state and federal governments from denying the right to vote to any male citizen because of race or previous condition of servitude. This allowed all male United States citizens the right to vote.

Chapter 17 Test, Form B

Matching
1. B
3. C
5. A
2. E
4. D

Multiple Choice
6. C
8. A
10. A
7. B
9. C

Document-Based Questions
11. C
12. D

Essay
13. The black codes were modeled on laws that had regulated free African Americans before the Civil War. The black codes trampled the rights of African Americans. Some laws allowed local officials to arrest and fine unemployed African Americans and make them work for white employers to pay off their fines. Other laws banned African Americans from owning or renting farms. One law allowed whites to take orphaned African American children as unpaid apprentices. To freed men and women and many Northerners, the black codes reestablished slavery in disguise.

Chapter 17 Test, Form C

Matching
1. A
3. C
5. B
2. E
4. D

Answer Key

Multiple Choice

6. D   8. B   10. A

7. C   9. A

Document-Based Questions

11. B

12. He believes it would promote military rule and force people to adopt principles and measures that they are opposed to and that are against the Constitution. He believes it is destructive.

Essay

13. Because of charges of corruption in the Grant administration and an economic depression, Democrats gained seats in the Senate and won control of the House of Representatives from the Republicans. The increased power of Democrats in Congress meant less commitment to Reconstruction and less support for African American rights.